CRYPTO FOR BEGINNERS

A SIMPLE NON-TECHNICAL GUIDE ON THE BLOCKCHAIN REVOLUTION AND CRYPTO INVESTING FOR CREATING MULTI-GENERATIONAL WEALTH

HUDSON LEE

This book is dedicated to my mom and dad,
For always standing behind me and helping me seeing the world from
different angles

CONTENTS

Introduction   xi

1. DISCOVERING THE CRYPTOCURRENCY WORLD   1
   Secret Blueprint for Cryptocurrency Discovery   2
   How Can you Benefit from Cryptocurrencies?   7
   Be Your Bank   7
   Financial Independence   8
   Freedom to Live Anywhere   8
   Freedom from Big Brother   9
   Ability to Earn Extraordinary Returns   9
   More Privacy   11
   No More Remittance Service Fees   12
   The Difference between Fiat and Crypto   13
   Currencies
   Crypto and Fiat Currency Accounts   13
   Crypto- and Fiat-Supported Credit/Debit Cards   14
   Blockchain Innovations   14
   Smart Contracts   14
   Decentralized Finance   15
   Decentralized Applications   16
   Non-Fungible Tokens (NFTs)   17
   Play-to-Earn Games (P2E Games)   17

2. HAVING THE RIGHT OPTICS ON THE   19
   CRYPTOCURRENCY WORLD
   What Makes Cryptocurrency So Important?   19
   History of Money   20
   What is Bitcoin?   26
   Are Bitcoin and Ethereum Real Money?   27
   What is Cryptocurrency?   27
   What are Stablecoins, and Why Are They Needed?   27
   Are Blockchains and Cryptocurrency the Same?   28
   Is Crypto a Ponzi Scheme?   29
   What Makes Crypto Valuable?   29
   What Can You Do with Cryptocurrency Besides   31
   Use It as Payment?

Do Only Bad People Use Cryptocurrency?   32
Is My Money Safe in Cryptocurrency?   32
Why Are There So Many Cryptocurrencies?   33
Is Now the Right Time to Get into Cryptocurrency?   34
Is Crypto a Bubble?   34
Mass Adoption of Cryptocurrency Has Not Yet Occurred   35

3. THE BLOCKCHAIN REVOLUTION IS MAKING IT ALL POSSIBLE   36
What is a Blockchain?   36
Why is It Called a Blockchain?   37
Blockchain Characteristics   37
Decentralized Nodes   38
Immutability   39
Transparency   40
Cryptography   40
Blockchain Security: 51% Attacks   41
Consensus Algorithms   42
Transaction Speed   43
The Blockchain Challenge: Decentralization and High TPS Rate   44
No Double-Spending   45
Governance   45
Blockchain Forks: Hard & Soft Forks   46
Communicating between Different Blockchains   49

4. THE ROADMAP TO CRYPTOCURRENCY OWNERSHIP   52
What is a Cryptocurrency Exchange?   52
Selecting the Best Centralized Crypto Exchange for You   53
Accessibility   53
Security   54
Insurance   54
Storage   54
Two-Factor Authentication   55
Larger vs. Smaller Cryptocurrency Exchanges   55
Exchange Fees   56
Liquidity   57
Listed Tokens   57
Educational Tools   58

Tax Information   58
Decentralized Crypto Exchanges   58
Everything You Wanted to Know about Crypto   60
Wallets
What is a Crypto Wallet?   60
Crypto Wallet Passwords and Secret Seed Phrases   61
Custodial vs. Non-Custodial Wallets   61
Private Keys   62
Public Keys   62
Public-Private Key Encryption   63
Single vs. Multi-Chain Wallets   63
Crypto Wallet Addresses   64
Types of Crypto Wallets   65
Creating an Account on a Centralized   68
Cryptocurrency Exchange

5. CASE STUDY – WHOLESOME BOUNTY   74
   GARDENERS AND THE BLOCKCHAIN
   REVOLUTION

6. BUILDING YOUR CRYPTOCURRENCY DEFENSES   83
   Cryptocurrency Scams Are on the Rise   83
   Fake Crypto Exchanges   84
   How to Protect Yourself   86
   Fake Crypto Wallets   86
   Hidden Wallets   87
   Pump-and-Dump Schemes   87
   Shilling Scam   89
   Phishing Scams   90
   Celebrity/Influencer Impersonators   91
   SIM Hack   92
   Asymmetrical Giveaways   94
   General Rules for Avoiding Having Your   95
   Cryptocurrency Stolen via Hacking or Scams
   Protecting Your Custodial Crypto Accounts,   95
   Private Keys, and Secret Seed Phrases
   2FA   95
   Hacking Email Accounts   96
   SIM Swapping   96
   Authenticator Apps   96
   Guidelines for Strong Crypto Wallet Passwords   97
   Generating Strong Passwords   98

7. HOW TO FIND CRYPTOCURRENCY GEMS   99
   Fundamental Analysis vs. Technical Analysis   99
   Cryptocurrency Fundamental Analysis (FA)   100
   Qualitative & Quantitative Analysis   101
   White Paper Review   107
   On-Chain Analysis   108
   Fundamental Analysis' 4 Basic Assumptions   110
   Technical Analysis (TA)   110
   Technical Analysis (TA) Tools   111
   General TA Tool Components   112
   Candlesticks   113
   Candlestick Strength   116
   Chart Patterns   118
   Bearish Candlestick Pattern   119
   Bullish Reversal Pattern   120
   Bearish Reversal Pattern   121
   Continuation Trend Pattern   122
   Support and Resistance Levels   122
   Breakout Pattern   123
   Other TA Tools   124
   Paper Trading   125
   Finding Your Needle in the Haystack   126
   Build Your Crypto Wealth Now!   126

8. STRATEGICALLY PROFIT FROM CRYPTOS AND   128
   THE KEYS TO CREATING YOUR MULTI-
   GENERATIONAL WEALTH
   What is Multi-Generational Wealth?   128
   Adopt a Long-Term Investment Game Plan   131
   Trading vs. HODLing   132
   HODL Your Way to Generational Wealth   134
   How to HODL   138
   Think Long-Term   138
   You Must Plant the Seeds of Wealth   138
   HODL-Worthy Cryptocurrencies   138
   Dollar-Cost Average Your Way into HODLing   139
   Be Prepared to Ride Out the Highs and Lows   140
   Cash on Hand   140
   Sell Targets for Profit-Taking   140
   Reinvest Your Profits   142
   Diversify Your Portfolio   143

What Not to Do When Investing in Cryptos 144
Decide to Take Action! 148

9. YOUR GUIDE ON CRYPTOCURRENCY TAXES 150
   The Internal Revenue Service and Crypto Taxation 151
   With Cryptocurrency Comes Tax Liability 151
   Crypto Tax Basics 152
   Taxable Crypto Transactions 153
   Potentially Taxable Crypto Transactions 155
   Tax-Free Crypto Transactions 156
   Prohibited Capital Gains Losses 157
   Full Investment Write-Off 157
   Tax Deductions on Crypto Sold at a Loss 157
   Unsettled Crypto Tax Issues 158
   Wash-Sale Rule & Its Risks 158
   Short-Term vs. Long-Term Capital Gains Tax 158
   Schedule
   General Crypto Tax Reporting Basics 160
   Paying Crypto Taxes 162
   Tax Forms You Need to Know 162
   Filing Your Crypto Taxes 164
   Manually Filing Your Crypto Taxes 164
   Using a Cryptocurrency Online Tax Preparation 165
   Software
   Manage Raw Cryptocurrency Transactional Data 165
   Create Your Cryptocurrency Master Portfolio 166

Conclusion 169
References 179

Thanks for Purchasing this Book!
We have a Free Gift for You!

Top Cryptocurrency Picks for Creating Your Multi-generational Wealth

- Three outstanding cryptocurrencies to invest in that are poised for incredible long-term returns 10X to even 1,000X return
- Get a simplified summary of each of these cryptocurrencies
- Noteworthy qualities of each of these cryptocurrency projects
- Understand why these cryptocurrencies are long-term winners
- How to buy these cryptocurrencies

Download Your Free Gift Now:

Visit https://hudsonleepublishers.com/MGW-COINS

OR scan the QR code below

INTRODUCTION

Cryptocurrency investing is either the most excellent investment and wealth opportunity available or the most significant scam since Bernie Madoff's Ponzi scheme.

You've been wondering whether it's worth it, but you have also been watching record numbers of people change their lives, fortunes, and futures by successfully investing in cryptocurrency. You also know that governments, banks, and financial institutions are making moves to accept and create their cryptocurrencies. So, if the most prominent players in local and global economies are moving into cryptocurrency, shouldn't you?

Well, that is why you are here. You are still on the fence about whether cryptocurrency investments suit you and what they can do for you. Here is an excellent place to be. Your questions get answered here, and you learn how to invest in crypto markets and limit potential losses intelligently.

How can this book help you?

With this eBook (or book), you can learn about the following:

- Cryptocurrency fundamentals
- Blockchain basics
- How to invest in cryptocurrency intelligently
- How to keep your cryptocurrency secure
- How to find the best crypto tokens for investment
- Different strategies investors use to analyze the performance of crypto tokens
- Trading strategies used by crypto investors
- How to maximize gains and minimize losses
- How to pay taxes on your crypto investments
- Plant seeds for multi-generational wealth

After reading this book, you will not be an expert on these topics. However, you will be able to listen to experts talk about these topics and understand them! Moreover, you will be able to converse with other investors about these topics and express your concerns about the crypto market without feeling unprepared. Even more importantly, you will be able to follow the social media sites, news media stories, podcasts, etc. that focus on cryptocurrency and blockchain technologies. This book provides an essential foundation that will enable you to become part of a developing financial system that is here to stay and changing our everyday lives.

"Who are *you* to teach me about cryptocurrency and blockchain technology?"

You don't want to waste your time reading the random thoughts of a writer who lacks the experience in and understanding of the crypto and blockchain world, do you? I understand. Time is a limited resource; we should use it wisely.

My name is Hudson Lee. I got into cryptocurrency several years ago. I was a successful stock investor and applied these skills to crypto investing. Furthermore, I performed technical analysis on market data and trading systems to determine if they could be the right solutions for institutional banks and thrive for years to come. This type of technical analysis, which determines the best technology to fulfill business needs, required years of experience and an in-depth understanding of low-latency and high-throughput architecture, functionality, resiliency, robustness, and code quality, as well as hours of rigorous validation testing.

Similarly, this skill set can provide insight into understanding the success of a blockchain. In short, I became a crypto investor after researching and analyzing the crypto market for other people. Over time, I realized that the market was profitable for investors and a fantastic way to plant the seeds of multi-generational wealth.

Satoshi Nakamoto, the famed pseudonym of the creator(s) of Bitcoin, wanted to democratize wealth accumulation. He also wanted to remove parasitic go-betweens who do nothing but provide the most basic services yet siphon off your funds while they are in transit from the sender to the receiver. The peer-to-peer network—the blockchain—moves cryptocurrency from one place to another. It crosses all borders, political systems, social systems, and religions. As a result, it is out of reach of third-party parasites and watchmen who have no business telling you what you can do with your money, where you can spend it, and when you can access it. How dare they do this anyway, right? It's *your* money!

Build Your Income and Wealth

After studying the equity markets for years, I took my knowledge and applied it to my finances. I wanted some of the mouthwatering profits that others were earning from investing in suitable crypto tokens at the right time. My system worked! Not only was I making higher profits than from my traditional investments, but I was building wealth faster and in a more secure environment than I had ever imagined could be done. My desire to share the potential of investing in blockchain technology grew steadily over time and ultimately blossomed into the book you are now reading.

Let's address all your reservations. Those of you with experience in investing might wonder if I wake up at night screaming in terror when there is a bear market (for those of you unfamiliar, a bear market is when all the money you invested starts to lose value very quickly and you're left with the difficult decision of whether to sell your investments or wait until the price of the investments goes back up). Well, I don't. I manage my crypto risks so I don't lose too much money or endanger my family, assets, or way of life. You can do it too. Crypto is not an all-or-none deal. It is an investment option that you can tailor to your lifestyle and financial needs. Whether you are a short- or long-term investor, you can get what you want from crypto and come out ahead.

Why I am Writing This eBook

Simply put, I want more people to get into the crypto market and make money. The more people who invest in the market and use cryptocurrency, the faster the crypto market can evolve and become more profitable, and the faster we can use crypto tokens like we use cash. When you and others invest in the crypto market and become crypto enthusiasts, other crypto investors benefit too. Unlike other forms of investments, the crypto world is not stacked with elite, rich, privileged people who seek to concentrate wealth in their little circle and let the rest of us have a few crumbs. No, the crypto world is something new and different. It is accessible to everyone, and everybody has a chance to create more income and wealth with it.

This book aims to help everyday people like you understand cryptocurrency and blockchain technologies—and not just know how they work but how you can invest in them, earn money, and build wealth for future generations. I have tried to explain these ideas to people one-on-one, and I continually see the fear, uncertainty, curiosity, and panicked looks on their faces as I introduce them to this world. Moreover, it is even worse to watch people latch onto crypto and make impulsive investment decisions that financially devastate them. You can avoid this FUD (fear, uncertainty, doubt) about cryptocurrency investing if you take the time to familiarize yourself with the ideas, their implementation, the pros and cons of the crypto market, and how you can take calculated risks when investing in it. This book exists to make that happen.

"What can crypto investing do for me?"

Crypto investing has led to some of the most amazing rags-to-riches, heartwarming stories ever told. However, my personal favorite is the one that I helped enable. Can you relate to this story?

My friend Janie (not her real name) needed money to pay for her son's private school tuition. But unfortunately, she wasn't just a little short of funds. Janie needed a year's worth of tuition or her son could not have the education she wanted him to have and that would hopefully afford him a better life situation.

Janie complained about her financial woes, and I proposed a solution. Yep, you guessed it: crypto investing. After working with me, Janie ran the numbers and figured out how much money she needed to earn in the crypto market to pay her son's tuition and the taxes on her crypto investments. Each crypto token granted has its personality and characteristics; we worked together to pick the crypto tokens that would give her the return she needed within the time frame required.

Finally, Janie's crypto tokens reached the market price levels necessary to reach her financial goal. She sold all her crypto holdings, and Janie's son attended his private school that year. Janie's investment returns paid her son's entire tuition before he started classes.

Crypto Investing vs. Gambling in Las Vegas

Crypto investing is not like going to Las Vegas and betting everything on a lucky turn of the dice (I'm not saying it can't feel like that, though). But no, it is like any other investment. You study the market, the assets available for purchase or trade, and make your move(s) when the time is right. The key is to remain dispassionate, rational, disciplined, and focused on your short- and/or long-term goals. Profitable returns are possible, and you can make them. Crypto millionaires and billionaires are doing it right now.

Nothing Worse than Regret

Investing in the upcoming blockchain revolution is your opportunity to learn about cryptocurrency and blockchain and what they can do for you. If you are willing to discover and understand it, you may be ready to change your life, fortune, and future by investing in it. This time will never come again. Find out if there is more that you can do for yourself and your family today.

CHAPTER 1
DISCOVERING THE CRYPTOCURRENCY WORLD

TAKE-HOME Message

Your mindset is critical to determining your success when you begin investing in crypto. If your perspective is off, you are significantly more likely to veer towards erroneous information, make bad investments, and lose money.

The Elephant in the Room

You are beginning your crypto journey. You may feel overwhelmed by everything you think you need to know about crypto. You hesitate to dive into crypto because you have reservations. Most people have resisted the desire to invest in crypto for the following reasons:

- Fear of losing money caused by bad experiences
- Fear of not being able to understand cryptocurrency

- Overwhelm due to current life situation
- Lack of time
- Too many responsibilities or other investments (i.e., too many irons in the fire)
- Comfort – your current financial situation is sufficient; why change it?
- You are ready to learn and are fearless but don't know how to start

SECRET BLUEPRINT FOR CRYPTOCURRENCY DISCOVERY

This book will teach you how to quickly increase your understanding of cryptocurrency without hours of technical study, jargon learning, and confusion. Before starting your crypto adventure, consider four key factors that will affect your success in implementing the 1-2-3-4 Simplify technique. The four factors are your decision, effort, purpose, and tribe.

Your Decision

It would be best to decide that you would make cryptocurrency work for you and serve your purposes. Understand that you have chosen to focus on one thing and ignore everything else when you decide. You use your free will to zero in on your top priority, making your crypto investing experience successful and profitable. Finally, crypto investing is always emotional. If you have been financially struggling and suffering from not meeting your needs, crypto investing will cause you emotional turmoil. With your free will, you decide to dial into the frequencies and emotions of successful investing and do not focus on fear, negativity, or bad past experiences.

When you begin your crypto journey, your mindset should be, "I will make cryptocurrency serve my financial purpose." Be clear on your decision and know that you have already decided what will happen in your future. In your mind, always think, "I decide that I will make cryptocurrency serve the financial purpose I want."

I highly recommend reading the book *The Law of Attraction* by Esther and Jerry Hicks to get a better understanding of how you can manifest things that you focus on consistently. The same concept can be applied here with your cryptocurrency discovery journey and your investments. You have to make the decision, focus on the decision, and put in the effort to make cryptocurrency investing work for you—and more so to make yourself feel the joy of having cryptocurrency work for you. Even with a simple trade that makes you an additional $100, you should feel that accomplishment to keep you motivated for your next profitable transaction.

Your Effort

After deciding, the next step is to commit to the effort required to master cryptocurrency investing. But first, you must commit to learning a little about cryptocurrency daily. So, your mindset must be, "I will take a little time every day to learn something new about cryptocurrency, and I will not give up." You will be amazed at how much you have learned over the months and years of studying crypto.

You must also acquire materials to help you learn what you want to know, which means stocking up on the videos, books, podcasts, newsletters, etc. that teach you what you want to learn in the way you want to learn it. Why? If the material is too complex, technical, dry, or whatever, you will soon lose your drive to learn about cryptocurrency because you will feel overwhelmed.

Ultimately, you must decide to keep encouraging yourself to

learn about the crypto world. Your passion should be to keep learning about crypto and making it serve your purpose. Don't give up on your mission to have crypto help you.

If you are reading this book, then you are halfway to making cryptocurrency investing work for you. This is because you already have taken the initiative and have the right mindset to start learning about cryptocurrency investments. And remember that you are at an incredibly early stage in the cryptocurrency world and are way ahead of the mass adoption period. Your focus now is to continue to learn about different crypto investment opportunities and ways to reduce losses. You should be proud that you have come down this path to be an early adopter of the revolutionary blockchain.

Your Purpose

Clarity of purpose is key to sustaining your effort and staying true to your decision. To begin this process, you must list the reasons why you want to invest in cryptocurrency. Many people choose to invest in cryptocurrency to do the following:

- Make new purchases, such as a car or new home
- Renovate their homes
- Pay for their children's educational fees / tuition
- Pay off debt (e.g., home mortgage, student loans, medical expenses)
- Start their businesses
- Diversify their investments
- Achieve individual financial sovereignty and freedom
- Generate monthly residual income
- Quit their jobs
- Generate multi-generational wealth

Your Tribe

Find your tribe! Your tribe is powerful and key to your success. Who is the tribe?

The tribe is a group of like-minded people who want to learn about cryptocurrency and share similar goals with you. You should meet at a designated time and place (in person or online) for 30 minutes to an hour twice a month or monthly. As a group, you and your tribe will encourage, support, and teach one another during your respective crypto journeys. Moreover, the members of your tribe can help you avoid potential problems, share experiences, and propose ideas that never would have occurred to you. Lastly, with your tribe, you will be shocked at how quickly you learn about crypto investing and trading.

Example: Effectiveness of a Tribe

If you want to be a real estate investor, you should join a real estate club. Even if you don't own any real estate or have plans to purchase any shortly, the club will provide excellent opportunities to learn about the industry and how to make money. Plus, when you are ready to buy your first piece of real estate, there will be people there to cheer you on and warn you about potential problems with your investment. Later, if you have issues with your real estate investment, there will be a room full of people to help you solve them. In this scenario, the wealth of knowledge, experience, and support in your real estate group will benefit you and everyone else in the group. It will make you more likely to succeed and less likely to make mistakes.

· · ·

1-2-3-4 Simplify Technique

1-2-3-4 Simplify is a comprehensive approach to pace yourself when getting into cryptocurrency and avoid getting overwhelmed rushing into decisions. This approach keeps everything as simple as counting: 1-2-3-4. To explore the crypto world and learn how to use it to achieve your goals, follow the 1-2–3-4 Simplify technique.

This technique is about not letting your impulsive gut reactions get the best of your decision-making process but instead considering information rationally and managing issues sequentially. For example, suppose a novice crypto investor gets 15 insider secrets that a crypto asset will either sharply drop in value or shoot up. In this case, he may make rash decisions and poorly thought-out actions based on his emotions.

The 1-2-3-4 Simplify technique prevents this by having you take the following steps before investing:

1. Ask yourself, "Do you know the technology behind this blockchain?"
2. Ask yourself, "Is this information from a trusted source?"
3. Ask yourself, "Can I afford to invest in this coin in my current situation?"
4. Ask yourself, "Do I have an exit strategy?"

The person who follows these steps will not rush in or out of the crypto market. One of the reasons people lose money in the crypto market is because they act with a herd mentality. If Person A and Person B did it, they think it is safe to do and a good idea. Successful investors must practice due diligence.

Also, simplifying the process to get clarity makes it easier to make the right decisions for yourself. For example, if someone tells you a hot trading tip, don't consider it valid until you ask yourself some questions and are satisfied with the answers. In this case, you would ask yourself the following questions:

1. Who is the source?
2. If the person heard it from a friend, where did the friend hear the information?
3. Are any of the information sources trustworthy?
4. Are any of the people spreading the information acting on it now?
5. Is this information supported by independent sources, market data, press releases, etc.?

HOW CAN YOU BENEFIT FROM CRYPTOCURRENCIES?

BE YOUR BANK

Cryptocurrency allows you to be your bank. When you have cryptocurrencies, you can use them to borrow money. In addition, your crypto tokens can be used as collateral, as loan money to other crypto holders with interest, and to make cross-border payments with no fee, utilizing the blockchain and your crypto tokens.

Let's look at some things you can do if you have cryptocurrency:

- You can borrow up to US$1 million from Coinbase, one of the world's largest cryptocurrency exchange platforms, using your Bitcoin (BTC) as collateral for the loan. Note that there is no credit check required for this service.
- You can get a peer-to-peer loan using your cryptocurrency as collateral. The lender will charge

you interest; however, there will be no credit check. These short-term loans have varying interest rates and can be immensely helpful for someone who needs quick money to close a deal.

FINANCIAL INDEPENDENCE

Cryptocurrency provides financial independence from your government, central bank, and regulatory agencies. Right now, some people cannot remove substantial amounts of their own money from their bank without an approval from a bank officer. Some people cannot send tens of thousands of dollars worldwide to start a business, help a friend, or pay their children's tuition fees without approval from a bank officer. Moreover, it can be frustrating to have your financial transactions delayed or stopped because they do not fit within the guidelines of a regulatory agency that doesn't even understand what you're doing.

The financial independence that cryptocurrency offers is your chance to decide *how* you will spend your money, *when* you will spend your money, and *with whom* you will spend your money. Additionally, it will give you 24/7 *access* to your money. Financial independence is possible and done privately using an electronic device and the password to your crypto wallet. It is liberating to know that you are in total control of your finances, money, and investments and can access your cash without asking anyone for permission.

FREEDOM TO LIVE ANYWHERE

Cryptocurrency can be accessed anywhere in the world at any time. All you need is an electronic device, access to the Internet, and access to the blockchain. If you want to redeem your crypto tokens, you can do that in many currencies worldwide. In addition, companies will assist you in saving your cryptocurrency and transferring it to different destinations. This service allows you to access your cryptocurrency even in a country that has banned a particular cryptocurrency.

With your cryptocurrency, you can reside from anywhere, travel anywhere, and live your best life without permission from anyone. Often, people's financial situations restrict where and how they can live by limiting their access to their finances. The use of cryptocurrency removes these hindrances and makes it possible for you to live and travel within your means, access your funds no matter what, and maintain financial security.

FREEDOM FROM BIG BROTHER

Satoshi Nakamoto created Bitcoin and released it to the public in 2009 because he wanted to democratize wealth accumulation. The best way to democratize wealth accumulation is to keep the government, banks, and financial institutions out of people's financial affairs. When Big Brother is watching you, it is challenging for you to act in your self-interest or to do things that upset the status quo. However, Big Brother is no longer part of the equation when using cryptocurrency.

Big Brother, his agencies, and his middlemen do not regulate your crypto transactions, your crypto investments, the redemption of your crypto tokens, or cryptocurrency movement around the globe. This flexibility gives you unfettered opportunities to do things that people working within the traditional financial system cannot do. Others must deal with excessive fees, financial regulations, and possible missed opportunities due to the incompetence and slow pace of Big Brother and fellow extortionists.

ABILITY TO EARN EXTRAORDINARY RETURNS

Over time, cryptocurrency has been the source of wealth for many crypto billionaires and millionaires. In addition, by investing in cryptocurrency, people have paid off their mortgages, student loans, credit card debt, and even their children's school fees. These people have amassed wealth, paid off debts, and reached other financial goals because cryptocurrency provides extraordinary returns on investment. When you manage your crypto assets well and protect yourself from downturns in the market, you can realize exceptional returns. You can also reinvest your returns and earn even more money.

The age of crypto has not passed. There will be more bear markets for people to make extraordinary returns. In those markets, good investors will be able to double—maybe even triple—the value of their crypto assets. As more people enter the crypto market, there will be more opportunities to invest and earn more significant returns, more ways to diversify your portfolio, and more cryptos to include in your portfolio.

There are multiple ways to earn money from investing in crypto aside from trading cryptocurrencies. Other investment vehicles include:

- **Crypto Stock Tokens** – Tokenized stocks are an exciting new way to invest in the market. Because they're created on blockchain-enabled platforms, tokenized stocks can be bought and sold 24/7 with minimal fees, compared with traditional stock exchanges. In addition, the value of these digital coins is derived directly from the underlying asset so that you can gain exposure to some of the largest companies in the world.
- **Crypto Derivatives (Future and Options Contracts)** – Derivatives in the traditional financial market consist of contracts that derive their value from an underlying asset. For example, cryptocurrencies have their derivatives where traders engage in derivative trades to speculate on changes in the price of a cryptocurrency. Derivatives enable traders to take positions on assets without holding those assets in the form of futures, perpetuals, and options.

- **Crypto Exchange-Traded Funds (ETFs)** – A cryptocurrency ETF is a fund that provides exposure to the price of one or more digital tokens. A cryptocurrency ETF tracks the price of one or more cryptocurrencies, allowing investors to capture changes in value without taking ownership of the asset. ETFs are traded on major exchanges and can be bought and sold for a market price like any other stock.
- **Crypto Exchange-Traded Products (ETPs)** – ETPs track an underlying asset or group of assets. They behave much like a stock and can be traded on an exchange. ETFs are the most popular ETPs. The most popular types of ETF are passively managed, so they typically carry lower fees than actively managed mutual funds.

In addition, as time passes, more investment opportunities are opening up that are directly crypto-related. These opportunities will allow you to earn money, improve your financial situation, diversify your portfolio, and get extraordinary returns on your crypto investments.

MORE PRIVACY

You conduct cryptocurrency transactions on a blockchain. Blockchains, specifically public blockchains, are known to have transparent ledgers. A transparent ledger means that the public can observe all the transactions occurring on the blockchain. However, the public does not identify who is involved in the transactions on its network. Thus, the public does not know the identities of the parties involved in the transactions on a public blockchain. Instead, long strings of undecipherable alphanumeric values hide the identities of the transacting parties.

Because the identities are hidden, your crypto transactions

are private. No one you know or do business with will know what you are doing, whom you are doing it with, or how much crypto was involved in the transaction. Undisclosed identity and this level of privacy are almost nonexistent in traditional markets. Cryptocurrency allows financial privacy in an era where surveillance is all around us and nearly impossible to escape.

NO MORE REMITTANCE SERVICE FEES

For people who want to send money to their family, friends, or others to provide funds to pay for emergency expenses, bills, or whatever, there is always a cost when using a service that will send the money quickly. Numerous third-party money transfer companies, like Western Union, will transfer money from you to someone else anywhere in the world within minutes to hours. However, these services charge transaction fees and require you to complete paperwork before you can send the money. In other cases, you may want to send someone money using a bank transfer—maybe because it's easier and you have a bank account. However, you will also have to pay transaction fees for the bank transfer. In addition, you may the transfer may not be completed for days—or, in some cases, more than a week!

Using the blockchain, you can transfer cryptocurrency to people anywhere globally, and those people will receive the transfer in less than a second to no more than an hour. Moreover, outside the fee charged for executing a transaction on the blockchain, there are no other remittance fees that you must pay. That means more money gets to the people who need it than when you use a money wiring service. Furthermore, to access the crypto tokens and send them to the receiver, the recipient does not have to have a bank account or present identification, making it easier for people to collect the crypto funds and use them immediately.

THE DIFFERENCE BETWEEN FIAT AND CRYPTO CURRENCIES

Cryptocurrencies and fiat currencies are both mediums of exchange, but they are different in several ways. The issuing and governance of fiat currency are dictated by central banks, while blockchain protocols, codes, and communities govern cryptocurrency. Fiat currency requires intermediaries to distribute its legal tender, whereas cryptocurrency relies on peer-to-peer consensus for "trustless" transactions. There are also technical differences between these digital assets: cryptocurrencies utilize a distributed ledger known as the blockchain to facilitate monetary transfers; fiat currency is transmitted using a banking network that operates a SWIFT messaging network infrastructure. An example of fiat currency is the paper money that we use in the United States today.

CRYPTO AND FIAT CURRENCY ACCOUNTS

Many online companies create crypto and fiat currency accounts that people can use daily. These accounts allow users to set up joint accounts where crypto tokens can be redeemed and put into a fiat account. So, for example, you can use fiat currency to buy crypto tokens, which you can then deposit into a crypto account.

In addition, these companies are increasingly allowing people to directly deposit their paychecks into these accounts and have their check funds converted to cryptocurrency. A few operations have even set up services where account holders can have bills automatically paid from their accounts. One of the best things about these services is that some offer account insurance. The account insurance is that if you do not have enough money in your fiat account to cover an expense, the company will redeem your cryptocurrency and use the saved funds to pay off the remainder of your costs posted.

CRYPTO- AND FIAT-SUPPORTED CREDIT/DEBIT CARDS

Crypto and fiat currency credit and debit cards exist! At this time, Visa has more than 50 different partners and connects its customers to more than 70 million merchants around the world. Visa and its partners allow Visa customers to use cryptocurrency and fiat currency to pay for their credit card purchases. This service is so popular that in the first two quarters of 2021, Visa processed more than US$1 billion worth of cryptocurrency payments.

Coinbase has a Coinbase card, which is a debit card. It allows holders to spend their crypto at any merchants in Visa's global network and earn rewards. The card is a marriage between traditional and blockchain finance. It seamlessly ties together the two worlds. The marriage of the two systems guarantees that cryptocurrency holders are not missing out on opportunities available to people using fiat currency. Over time, these services will expand, build on each other, and offer users more rewards and options. Additionally, crypto cards' increased services and features make them more attractive and competitive than traditional credit and debit cards.

BLOCKCHAIN INNOVATIONS

Blockchain technology, particularly the Ethereum blockchain, has been the source of impressive technological innovations. Moreover, these technologies continue to advance and become more accepted and trusted by an ever-increasing community of network users. This section will look at some of the most notable blockchain innovations and why they are helpful to you.

SMART CONTRACTS

Smart contracts are self-executing contracts that do not use third parties. Instead, you create smart contracts by using computer code. The parties to the contract decide what conditions and terms must be met before payments for services and goods are transferred between them.

Some people prefer to use smart contracts rather than traditional contracts because they do not require the services of lawyers, accountants, auditors, or any other specialized professionals after the contract has been coded and executed.

Most of the costs associated with these contracts you incur while creating the contract. People who use smart contracts must spend a lot of money at the beginning of the contract process. Then, they must find expert programmers and lawyers who can work with programmers. Finally, the two must work together to distill a legal contract's language down into a form you that can be replicated in computer code. All of this takes time, effort, and skill.

Smart contracts are non-negotiable and inflexible, and you cannot adjust them after their execution. Therefore, any mistakes made during the programming of a smart contract can have horrific consequences for the parties involved. So, it pays to get the best people you can find to do this job.

Smart contracts also have severe limitations, such as being non-negotiable, unalterable, immutable, and difficult to code with legality. Overall, smart contracts are stringent and can make it challenging to maintain good business relationships in a volatile, unstable, or changing business climate.

DECENTRALIZED FINANCE

Decentralized Finance (DeFi) is the general term used to refer to banking and trade-related activities performed on the blockchain, primarily on the Ethereum blockchain. These activities include borrowing, lending, buying insurance, trading crypto assets, trading derivatives, and trading stock tokens.

When done on the blockchain, these financial activities are performed faster, with no third-party intermediaries or regulatory authorities overseeing their execution. Like a crypto payment transfer on the blockchain, DeFi transactions are peer-to-peer transactions.

Blockchain users on networks using DeFi apps can access the apps and engage in DeFi transactions. Some advantages of using the blockchain are that there are no transaction-related applications/forms to complete, no accounts to open, no brokers or agents to hire, and no approval process. It is, in fact, a very streamlined process that allows the blockchain user to conduct financial activities in private.

DECENTRALIZED APPLICATIONS

Decentralized applications (dApps) can run on blockchains or on peer-to-peer-networks (e.g., Tor, BitTorrent, Popcorn Time, Bitmessage). Peer-to-peer networks are those in which transactions are between two users on the internet with no intermediaries involved. As an example of a *centralized* transaction, if you wanted to book a ride on Uber, then the Uber company would be involved as a third-party intermediary. But peer-to-peer transactions have no third-party authority. Not only are dApps peer-to-peer transactions, but the data transacted is also stored on the blockchain, which means there is an immutable ledger to record all the transactions. We'll go over all the unique qualities of the blockchain later in this book.

dApps' user interfaces look identical to those found on websites and mobile apps. They also use smart contracts to manage payments and other transactions on the app. dApps can run multiple smart contracts simultaneously.

You can use dApps in finance, medicine, gaming, governance, and file storage. They are like the software programs that we use every day. The primary difference between dApps and software programs is that the dApps run on the blockchain, with no centralized location and intermediaries. In addition, dApps are less vulnerable to attacks than software run on a centralized system.

NON-FUNGIBLE TOKENS (NFTS)

Non-fungible tokens (NFTs) are electronic tokens that provide evidence of ownership of a unique item. NFTs are tokenized things you can purchase. For example, you can buy NFTs of art, music, videos, virtual real estate, legal documents, GIFs, tweets, car deeds, and other collectibles. NFTs' value comes from their scarcity due to a limited number of authorized NFTs sold to the public. You can find evidence or proof of an NFT's authenticity in its metadata. The NFT's metadata contains its creation date, creator information, and title of ownership.

NFTs are not interchangeable with cryptocurrencies (e.g., Ether, Bitcoin, XRP). Each NFT is unique and has a unique identifier. Your passcode (i.e., private key) is your proof that you own your NFT. Also, each NFT has a creator's public key. The creator's public signature (i.e., public key) proves that a specific person/entity created the NFT. The signature may be necessary if it affects the value of the NFT. For example, if the creator of an NFT already produced some high-value NFTs, then other NFTs from this creator will likely also have a higher value.

Although anyone can copy NFTs (they are strictly computer code), some people attribute immense value to owning them. The most common analogy to explain this thinking is that anyone can buy a counterfeit copy of a Picasso painting. Still, only one person can own and display the authentic Picasso painting.

PLAY-TO-EARN GAMES (P2E GAMES)

Play-to-Earn (P2E) games are dApps on a blockchain, primarily the Ethereum blockchain. People can earn crypto tokens while playing these games, and the tokens can store the tokens earned during the P2E games in the players' crypto wallets. Crypto wallets are electronic locations where you can store crypto tokens. To play a P2E game, the player must have a crypto wallet.

Some P2E games permit players to bet on game tournaments, matches, and player rankings. Today, some people play P2E games to earn side income. Some P2E games require players to pay a fee to join the fun. Others, especially newer ones, allow players to join the game, but they must pay for game supplies with the game's native crypto tokens if they want to participate.

CHAPTER 2
HAVING THE RIGHT OPTICS ON THE CRYPTOCURRENCY WORLD

TAKE-HOME Message

Cryptocurrency is the latest evolution of money. Blockchain technology has made it possible to use cryptocurrency in borderless, trustless, peer-to-peer transactions. In addition, it opens up a wide variety of alternative transactions that you can perform outside of the traditional financial system.

WHAT MAKES CRYPTOCURRENCY SO IMPORTANT?

Cryptocurrency gives the average person true financial sovereignty and wealth. As this technology evolves, it will create tremendous benefits for people for generations. The people who benefit from it will be the ones who realize its income-generating opportunities and invest in it at the right time. Furthermore, as more people invest in cryptocurrency, it will gain momentum and be propelled forward in society. As society gradually embraces cryptocurrency and realizes its true potential and power, it will become ubiquitous. Individuals who want financial independence and to create multi-generational wealth will be better served financially by investing in cryptocurrency.

Currency's Definition

In essence, money is a common way to price the work, productivity, and value of people and their things. Plus, currency is what our society agrees to accept as a medium of payment for goods and services. So, the money is given value, and the community then assesses the value of its goods and services using the socially accepted currency.

HISTORY OF MONEY

Monetary systems have evolved from bartering to digital currency. Let's look at how currency has graduated from exchanging your services and trading goods to sending electronic data from an electronic device across the Internet.[4]

Bartering

Under the barter system, which many people worldwide still use, people can get goods and services by exchanging other goods and services. For example, if a shoemaker wants a new wooden table for his home, he can offer to supply the village carpenter with enough shoes to pay for the wooden table.

The problem with this system is that people are limited to the goods and services they can provide to others. Or they must go through a series of different transactions before they can get something the other person wants and exchange it for what they want from that person. For example, maybe the shoemaker does not wish for shoes or need them, in our case. But, on the other hand, perhaps the shoemaker would like a cow in trade. So, the shoemaker must find someone who will exchange a cow for his shoes, or he may enter into a series of transactions that ultimately result in him getting a cow. Then, after receiving the cow, he exchanges it for the wooden table he wants for his home.

Natural Objects

Some societies have been able to move away from the bartering system. These early societies instead used natural objects as a form of currency. They used things like cowrie shells and whales' teeth. These natural objects were given a specific value and could be used to purchase goods and services. They functioned as currency because they were a form of payment accepted by everyone in exchange for other things.

Sovereign Nation's Currency

Over time, sovereign nations chose not to use natural objects and moved away from the bartering system. They did this by issuing their own currencies. The currency often had a king, queen, or prince's face printed on it, and the nation's government valued and accepted it as currency within its borders. This money was backed by the country's reputation, assets, credit, and reserves.

The problem with this currency was that it was only as good as the nation's credit and reputation. Therefore, there were concerns about trading it or purchasing goods and services outside the country. In addition, this problem worsened if the government was at war, in a dire financial situation, or facing political instability.

. . .

Metals

When societies realized the potential and value of metals, they started to use them as forms of payment. Metals were not only valuable as methods of payment, but you could use them to create weapons of war, cooking supplies, and shoes for horses.

Society derived the value of the money itself from the metals' actual use in the community. The utility of money matters, because when goods and services are valued using metal (e.g., iron, silver, copper), the metal's value is correlated to its value in society, particularly its importance to the government and military. For example, when war debts had to be paid by the country or the government was preparing for war, the government required the kingdom's people to contribute their metals (e.g., gold, silver, copper) to the government's war effort or debt repayment.

Metal Coins

Instead of just exchanging bits or chunks of metal, governments decided to create metal coins. Governments made specific metals with particular values in that society into coins. People were then able to exchange coins for goods and services. We know this was quite convenient for some societies because coin minters made holes in the center of the coins so that people could easily carry them on strings from place to place.

The coins were easier to transport, hide, secure, and value than various pieces of metal that people managed to acquire. They were also easier to exchange across different kingdoms. People in other domains could evaluate and assess the value of a metal and decide what it was worth, in terms of goods and services in their kingdom. In short, which domain created the metal coin was not necessary, only the kinds of metal used in the coins. Moreover, these metal coins could also be melted down and used to make pots, horseshoes, swords, armor, and other items the kingdom might need.

Coins became a vast improvement over the bartering system, natural objects, and metal (in general), but they had a significant drawback: people knew how to counterfeit coins. People made counterfeit metal coins and exchanged them for goods and services. The people doing this used inferior metal or other tricks to make their coins look and feel authentic. Consequently, merchants and the public had to be incredibly careful when receiving and exchanging metal coins.

Paper Money Backed by Gold

Later, governments began issuing paper money. Paper money was lighter, easier to carry, easier to hide, easier to secure, and broadcasted the sovereignty of a government. Therefore, people governed by the government would accept paper money in exchange for goods and services. Initially, the government did not back paper money with gold. Instead, the government approved paper money by its word that issued the money. In short, the government said the money had a particular value, and the government told the citizens to accept the paper money in exchange for goods and services. The problem with this system was that it did not work well when buying goods and services in other countries. It was also problematic if the country that issued the money had political and socioeconomic problems or if the future of the country's government was in question.

In the late 1800s, governments decided to back their currency with gold. Gold-backed paper money was much easier to exchange with other governments, and countries more widely accepted gold-backed paper money than paper money that countries did not back with gold. Why? Because, at that time, if you had gold-backed paper money, you could take it to a bank or financial institution and exchange the paper money for its gold equivalent. Gold-backed paper money made people feel more secure about the value of their goods and services, and the value of the paper money and made it much easier to make international trades.

Fiat Currency – Paper Money without the Gold Standard

Around the 1930s, some countries decided to leave the gold standard. These countries wanted to increase the amount of money in circulation but not have to increase their gold reserves. In essence, countries were printing unbacked money. By the 1970s, all nations had abandoned the gold standard. However, governments and banks do keep fractional gold reserves. What are fractional reserves? Fractional reserves are when only a fraction of the currency's value in circulation is backed by gold. To be blunt, it does not support all the money in circulation.

This new paper money was unbacked and referred to as fiat currency. The issue with fiat currency is that governments can issue new paper money whenever they want, but its value is unsecured. So, as governments print more paper money, the value of their cash declines. For example, suppose there is a rapid decline in the value of the capital. In that case, the society will experience inflation, and the people using that money will quickly realize that they have less buying power than before inflation.

Credit Cards

· · ·

Financial institutions introduced credit cards in the first half of the 20th century. Initially, credit cards were for the rich, famous, well-connected, and elite. However, they were made available to other segments of society over time. Credit cards attract people to pay for goods and services using the credit extended to them by a credit card company. The credit card company will pay their bills, understanding that the credit card owners will pay the money back to the credit card company.

Over the years, credit cards have become a very lucrative business for many credit companies. In the late 20th century, many credit card companies began to make their cards available to lower-income people who could not afford low-interest credit cards. Instead, they were offered high-interest credit cards with low balances. These low-income households often use credit cards to pay for basic living expenses, entertainment, and emergencies. These households use credit cards to cover basic living expenses. Unfortunately, these households' inability to make enough money to pay their living expenses has led many into credit card debt. Unfortunately, the many people who take out these high-interest and prepaid credit cards to pay their living, school, emergency, and holiday expenses have no real plan to pay the money back.

Digital Money (Digitized Currency, Cryptocurrency)

The latest evolution of money is digital money. Cryptocurrency is the first form of digital money created as a medium for payment. The original cryptocurrencies, Bitcoin (BTC) and Ethereum (ETH) are unbacked by assets but gain value based on their utility. However, some cryptocurrencies are backed by fiat currency, commercial paper, commodities, precious metals, real estate, etc.

Cryptocurrency should not be confused with digitized fiat

currency. At this time, the US, China, and other nations are developing their digitized currency. The digitized currency is essentially electronic fiat currency. It has the same value and is as trustworthy as paper money. A government, central bank, or some other kind of institution controls this digitized fiat currency. However, it is no more reliable or secure than holding fiat money. Remember, whatever happens to fiat money also happens to digitized fiat money.

WHAT IS BITCOIN?

Bitcoin was the first cryptocurrency ever created and released to the public. It was designed and distributed to the public by the pseudonymous Satoshi Nakamoto in 2009. The demand for Bitcoin establishes the value for Bitcoin. Therefore, the higher the need for it, the higher its price.

Ethereum, launched in 2015, was the second cryptocurrency created and released to the public. It was co-created by Vitalik Buterin, Gavin Wood, Charles Hoskinson, Anthony Di Lorio, and Joseph Lubin. The Ethereum blockchain is far more versatile than Bitcoin's blockchain. It has introduced the world to smart contracts, decentralized apps, blockchain games, play-to-earn games, a more dynamic metaverse, and decentralized finance.

Moreover, Ethereum can work with many other blockchains. In addition, Ethereum's native token, ETH, unlike BTC, is more than just a way to store value. You can use ETH as a payment, investment, source of passive income (e.g., mining, staking), and medium of exchange between different crypto tokens.

ARE BITCOIN AND ETHEREUM REAL MONEY?

The answer to this question is that it depends. It depends on how you define real money. If real money is a medium of payment that you can use to pay for things you want or to achieve your financial goals, then yes, it is real money. However, if real money is a currency you can touch and feel and is accepted as a form of payment by all businesses, banks, financial institutions, and governments, then, no, it is not real money. *Alternative* money better describes Bitcoin and Ethereum.

WHAT IS CRYPTOCURRENCY?

Cryptocurrency is a digital currency secured by cryptography, making it difficult, if not impossible, to counterfeit. A cryptocurrency is a form of cryptography because no information connects the transactions to the transacting parties when used in transactions on the blockchain. Therefore, cryptocurrency's significant attraction and benefit are that you can anonymously conduct blockchain transactions because crypto's cryptographic nature prevents people not involved in your transaction from knowing what you have done.

WHAT ARE STABLECOINS, AND WHY ARE THEY NEEDED?

Stablecoins are crypto tokens that have a set value. The value of stablecoins is the asset's value (backed by the US Dollar [USD], gold, silver, commodities, or real estate). The reserves and assets backing stablecoins act as a guarantee that you can redeem them for a specific value.

Stablecoins were needed to entice more businesses and people to want to use cryptocurrency. Cryptocurrency is well known for being volatile and having its values suddenly rise or fall. Therefore, companies wanted to ensure that the crypto payment they agreed to would have a consistent weight. Stablecoins have constant values and are not volatile. Their existence in the crypto market has made it possible for more businesses and people to engage in crypto transactions with less fear that they will lose money if the crypto market declines. After all, a stablecoin's value never changes, regardless of what happens in the crypto market.

If businesses accept stablecoins as payment for their goods and services, they know they will receive a specific amount of money when redeeming the coins in fiat currency. Furthermore, stablecoins make cryptocurrency more appealing to the private sector, public sector, and individuals. They are an entry point into the crypto market. They are more attractive and less intimidating because they do not seem as risky and threatening as traditional cryptocurrencies like Bitcoin, Ethereum, Cardano, and XRP.

In addition, stablecoins are a terrific way to move your wealth out of the traditional economic system and into the digital one. Owners of stablecoins maintain the value of their assets, but they can access them from anywhere. More importantly, these transfers you can execute without government approval, government interference, and the payment of government fees.

ARE BLOCKCHAINS AND CRYPTOCURRENCY THE SAME?

No, blockchains are platforms on which users can conduct cryptocurrency transactions. Cryptocurrency is the payment used by people who want to execute transactions on a blockchain. For example, the Bitcoin blockchain uses Bitcoin (BTC) as its medium of payment. However, the Ethereum blockchain accepts its native token, Ether (ETH), and any Ethereum blockchain–compatible crypto tokens. Therefore, you can transact on the Ethereum blockchain with various compatible tokens.

IS CRYPTO A PONZI SCHEME?

A Ponzi scheme is a fraudulent investment that promises high returns to investors at minimal risk. It operates by paying its early investors high returns using the investment capital collected from later investors. However, the Ponzi scheme will eventually fall apart when not enough new investors come in, and the fraudsters cannot continue paying the excessively high returns promised to their investors.

Some argue that crypto is a Ponzi scheme because as more investors buy crypto tokens, the tokens increase in value. For those interested in short-term trading, this may be true. However, it does not qualify as a Ponzi scheme because prospective investors know that crypto trading is high-risk and can be incredibly speculative. Also, while investors have previously received stratospheric returns on their crypto investments, such returns are not promised or guaranteed. Instead, they are simply something many investors hope for when buying crypto tokens, especially newly launched ones.

Crypto enthusiasts will argue that cryptocurrencies are admittedly high-risk investments that operate in a volatile market and do not fall under the same scope and guise as a Ponzi scheme. Moreover, crypto traders must contend with changing market regulations, government restrictions, and other factors that allow investors to earn high returns by investing in high-risk crypto assets. Therefore, none of those mentioned above are characteristics of a Ponzi scheme.

WHAT MAKES CRYPTO VALUABLE?

Distinct kinds of crypto tokens have different valuations. In this regard, not all cryptocurrencies are created equal. For example, would you rather own 10 Bitcoins or 10 Dogecoins?

Of course, you would opt-in for 10 Bitcoins over 10 Dogecoins, the reason being the overall value you are getting with Bitcoin. Firstly, at the time of this writing, a single Bitcoin is worth $40,000 USD, and Dogecoin is worth less than 10 cents. Also, the Bitcoin cryptocurrency has its own blockchain, and Dogecoin is hosted on the Ethereum Blockchain. Bitcoin has proven itself as a store of value and has a long track record to show for it, while Dogecoin is basically a meme coin that only grows in value due to social media trends or news.

Moreover, not all crypto tokens maintain their value over time, increase in value over time, and exist for years. A cryptocurrency may become valuable if it meets most of the following conditions:

- Serves a purpose
- Meets a need
- Is supported by a community
- Is heavily invested in by founders
- Generates a high demand
- Is designed well
- Has a blockchain
- Is multi-functional
- Is scarce (limited quantity available)

Let's look at two different cases:

Bitcoin and Ether are valuable cryptocurrencies because there is a limited supply of them. In addition, they have specific uses; many people want to own them and conduct transactions, have high status in the crypto world, and have their blockchains. However, most crypto tokens on the market do not have the same characteristics as Bitcoin and Ether. Therefore, the value of these other cryptocurrencies will not behave over time like Bitcoin and Ether.

In contrast, there are currently thousands of crypto tokens on the market. Unfortunately, most of them have extraordinarily little value. Furthermore, the likelihood is that as blockchains evolve, there will be a divest of 95% of the tokens in circulation ten years from now. So, not all crypto tokens have value; not all of them will increase in value or be around for years to come.

WHAT CAN YOU DO WITH CRYPTOCURRENCY BESIDES USE IT AS PAYMENT?

With cryptocurrency, you have the ability to do many things, depending on the kind of cryptocurrency that you own. In general, you may be able to do some of the following with your crypto tokens:

- Mine them – Use your computer to earn cryptocurrencies by helping the blockchain process transactions
- Stake them – Use your cryptocurrencies and invest them to earn interest
- Loan them with interest to others
- Get crypto loans and use them as collateral
- Use them to earn passive income from liquidity pools
- HODL them – Hold On for Dear Life them (Hold them for long-term investments)
- Engage in short- and/or long-term trading
- Invest in crypto to derivatives
- Invest in crypto-based CFDs (contracts for differences), ETFs (electronically traded funds), ETPs (exchange-traded products), and crypto stock tokens
- Gamble with them (e.g., crypto casinos)
- Play blockchain games
- Use them in decentralized applications
- Use them (as a form of payment) in smart contracts
- Use them (as a form of payment) in decentralized financial transactions

DO ONLY BAD PEOPLE USE CRYPTOCURRENCY?

Let me ask you a question: Do only bad people use paper money? The obvious answer to that is no. Yet, you know that many people are doing illegal things with paper money. Has that stopped you from using paper money as a form of payment? No, it hasn't. The next question I want to ask you is: How do you define *bad people*? If you ask if people can use cryptocurrency for illegal transactions and money laundering, then the answer is yes. Suppose you ask if people use cryptocurrency to get around government sanctions, laws, and other restrictions. The answer is still yes. However, people also use paper money, gold, precious metals, and gemstones to do those things. So, why would you think that cryptocurrency should be an exception to this behavior? Lastly, most people using cryptocurrency use it as a form of payment in completely legal transactions.

IS MY MONEY SAFE IN CRYPTOCURRENCY?

Is your money safe as fiat currency? Is your money safe in your local bank?

If you have been watching the collapse of different economies worldwide (e.g., Turkey, Venezuela, Lebanon), you would know that having paper money does not guarantee that the value of your money is safe, protected, or reliable. Your money is not secure unless you own some minerals, precious metals, or valuable gemstones. And, even with precious metals, minerals, and gems, their value is what someone is willing to pay for them when you are doing the exchange. For example, if all the banks collapse, there is war, and people are starving, the value of food will surpass the value of your precious metal, minerals, and gemstones. Cryptocurrency is risky. You must accept its risks if you want to be a crypto investor. You can shield yourself from the dangers, but the stakes will still be there. For instance, hackers can try to access your crypto wallet or exchange account and attempt to steal your crypto coins. You could also lose your private keys and be unable to access your crypto tokens. At any time, the value of your crypto tokens could crash and never recover.

Needless to say, these risks are similar to someone stealing your credit card number and using it to make fraudulent charges. But with cryptocurrency in your possession, there is no customer service fraud to dispute these charges or withdrawals. Later in the book, we will learn about how to safely secure your cryptocurrencies so that this would most likely never happen. But you should understand and be aware of these when you invest in cryptocurrency.

The advice given to all crypto investors is never to invest more than you can afford to lose. Or, put another way, never invest more than you can comfortably walk away from with no regrets.

WHY ARE THERE SO MANY CRYPTOCURRENCIES?

Each cryptocurrency has a unique value that serves a specific purpose and caters to certain types of businesses or interests. So, people create them to fill those niches (e.g., privacy, fast transaction processing, gaming tokens). Other cryptocurrencies are joke or meme coins (e.g., Dogecoin). Still, other cryptocurrencies are poorly designed and launched as investment scams.

You should know that crypto scams increase at least tenfold each year. The extraordinary increase in crypto scams is due to the large amounts of money in the crypto market and its abundance of inexperienced investors. Unfortunately, the crypto world is an irresistible target for scammers and fraudsters. Many people are eager to invest in crypto assets, yet they cannot discern legitimate investments from outright scams.

IS NOW THE RIGHT TIME TO GET INTO CRYPTOCURRENCY?

Yes, this is a perfect time to get into crypto. If the prices of crypto are running fairly high as you are thinking of investing in cryptocurrency, remember that the mass adoption period has not yet occurred and if you make the right cryptocurrency picks based on the fundamental analysis we will discuss in later chapters, you'll be ready for the massive returns when cryptocurrency mass adoption takes place. Remember, cryptocurrency is gambling, and with gambling, there are inherent risks, but if you start to understand how revolutionary blockchain technology is and its impact on society, you can rest assured you are investing in a sound technology. If the prices of the cryptocurrency market are currently down, this is an even a better reason to buy cryptocurrency.

IS CRYPTO A BUBBLE?

The crypto market has experienced several bubbles. At the time of this writing, the crypto market is correcting itself. When the market corrects itself, the prices of crypto tokens drop markedly. The sudden decline in crypto tokens' valuations scares people. The naysayers use it as proof that the crypto market is a scam. However, it is well known that most modern markets go into bubbles when they are hot (e.g., mortgage, real estate, dotcom, savings, and loans).

Suppose you ask me if the cryptocurrency market will disappear when the current bubble bursts. The answer is no. The market is doing a price correction. After the price correction completes, the market will still exist, and people will still invest in it and earn high yields.

The cryptocurrency market is like the Internet in 1990. It's hot, sexy, exciting, and flush with cash. Unfortunately, it's also an overheated market fueling overheated imaginations and lots and lots of greed. Like the dotcom crash cleared away all the bad and poorly performing web companies, crypto bubble bursts wash away the poorly performing crypto tokens and leave behind the high-quality, high-performing crypto tokens.

MASS ADOPTION OF CRYPTOCURRENCY HAS NOT YET OCCURRED

Although you can hear and read about cryptocurrency everywhere, it has not yet been integrated into traditional economies worldwide. A small percentage of people and well-capitalized businesses have invested in cryptocurrency. Growth opportunities and innovation attracted these businesses to it because it was new and had potential. Others saw the potential for great returns and that it had a future. Lately, many institutional investors and governments are now investing in it because they see it as a competitor. Still, overall investment in cryptocurrency is relatively tiny compared with other investments.

Note, rates of integration into local economies vary from region to region and, within regions, from country to country. Therefore, you will find, across the world, that populations differ in terms of their acceptance of cryptocurrency as a viable form of payment, a worthwhile investment, and as something that will continue to be a part of their economic system in the foreseeable future.

CHAPTER 3
THE BLOCKCHAIN REVOLUTION IS MAKING IT ALL POSSIBLE

TAKE-HOME **Message**

Before investing in cryptocurrency, you should understand the essential parts of a blockchain. As your knowledge of the blockchain grows, it will help you compare and evaluate distinct types of blockchains.

WHAT IS A BLOCKCHAIN?

A blockchain is like a digital ledger that publicly displays all the anonymous transactions processed and logged in a permanent digital record. It is similar to the ledger used for your checkbook. The ledger is the record section where you record your debits and credits.

Blockchain transactions are only between the sender and receiver of the payment and are known as peer-to-peer (P2P) transactions. There are no third parties involved in a P2P transaction. P2P transactions are trustless because no third parties supervise the transaction; it has no trustees.

The blockchain handles the entire transaction without the

assistance of any intermediaries. The trustless transaction gives participants independence from third-party oversight, governmental regulation, and censorship by parties not involved in the transaction.

WHY IS IT CALLED A BLOCKCHAIN?

Let's look at this from the perspective of Bitcoin's and Ethereum's original blockchains. When the programmers launched the blockchains, miners would create blocks of transactional data by solving complex mathematical equations. Miners are simply people who run a computer program to allow transactions to occur on the blockchain. The first miner to solve the equation won the right to process the next set of transactions.

Miners store the transactions in blocks. A block is like a USB memory stick with limited memory. Miners can only keep as many transactions as will fit within the block's memory. So, miners must select from the memory pool (mempool) a pool of transactions submitted for execution that will be processed and stored in the block.

The miner processes the transactions for the miner's block, and when finished, the miner adds their block to the most recently completed block. All the blocks have time and date stamps. This chain of blocks filled with transactional data is called the blockchain.

BLOCKCHAIN CHARACTERISTICS

In this section, you will review the essential characteristics of a blockchain. These characteristics make blockchains an incredible technological innovation that revolutionizes the world of finance and, ultimately, our everyday lives.

DECENTRALIZED NODES

Blockchains operate 24 hours a day, seven days a week and lack a central processing location. Furthermore, blockchain nodes are spread over many computers worldwide. Blockchain networks exist globally, meaning the government or other authoritative bodies cannot simply shut them down. Moreover, the nodes process P2P transactions, and no one oversees them; they are trustless transactions. In addition, if there are problems in one part of the network, other computers can continue to process network transactions. The computers on a blockchain network are called nodes. There are two types of nodes: full nodes and light nodes.

Full nodes have a complete copy of the blockchain and can add new blocks to the blockchain. The full node acts independently and is located anywhere in the world. Since they can all process transactions for the blockchain, governments can never shut down the blockchain. It operates independently of governments, regulatory agencies, police authorities, and any other form of interference found in a traditional financial system. Moreover, no one outside the blockchain can stop or censor the transaction before or during its execution.

Light nodes are partial nodes that do not have access to the entire blockchain. Instead, light nodes restrict access to regions of the blockchains. Blockchains use light nodes to increase the transaction processing speed of the blockchain. After a light node has processed a block, it sends the block to a full node. The full node then checks the work done by the light node before adding the block to the blockchain.

Besides having full and light nodes, blockchains employ numerous security personnel who work to keep the blockchain safe, secure, and reliable. Their primary purpose is to look for sketchy transactions, malicious conduct, and questionable behavior on the network. If they suspect any of these things, they alert other network personnel. When alerted, the network personnel investigate the suspicious behavior and transactions.

If the watchdogs are correct, the blockchain rewards them with native tokens. In addition, the blockchain punishes users engaging in illegal, malicious, and corrupting conduct. The punishment can range from having their staked tokens seized to being banned from the network.

Moreover, if the person punished was supported by others (e.g., using borrowed crypto tokens to qualify as a node), those supporting him are punished. Anyone caught facilitating, supporting, coordinating, or otherwise enabling inappropriate conduct on a blockchain will be penalized by the blockchain.

IMMUTABILITY

The blocks added to the blockchain also have time and date stamps included in the newly minted block before it has added the block to the blockchain. Furthermore, all full nodes have copies of the entire blockchain, and the full nodes must agree when the blockchain adds a new block. Because all the nodes on a blockchain must have identical records, the blockchain is considered immutable.

If there are differences between the records kept by the full nodes, then there is an immediate investigation into the matter. The transactions in question are suspended or delayed until the problem with the blockchain is understood and resolved. If the block contains questionable transactions, the blockchain does not execute the transactions. If there are no other problems, transactions will have to be resubmitted for approval and reprocessed by the blockchain.

This unchanging, unalterable public ledger gives the blockchain its reputation as a trustworthy network. The immutability of its record is something absent in traditional financial systems.

Technically, someone or a group can substitute one block for another block in a blockchain. However, replacing blocks on the blockchain would involve many people who need to plan, coordinate, and replace many blocks simultaneously, decreasing the likelihood of this happening. In addition, the timing of the block substitution would have to be perfect. Thus, it is almost impossible to change blockchain records once the blockchain cements the block.

TRANSPARENCY

Anyone with a computer and access to the internet can see the blockchain's public transactions. Even non-transacting parties can view the transaction on the blockchain, but more importantly, the blockchain does not disclose the identities of the transaction parties. However, the anonymity of the transacting parties does not obscure that the public can see their transactions.

CRYPTOGRAPHY

Cryptography on the blockchain enables its transacting parties to remain hidden from the public. Crypto wallets have addresses not connected to their owners' personal information. Furthermore, the private keys needed to access cryptocurrency do not link to their owner's personal information. Therefore, you have a payment system that is encoded from beginning to end.

Suppose you use a centralized crypto exchange (CEX) for your transactions. In that case, the CEX will have collected some personal information from you before it lets you register an account on its platform. In this case, the CEX can, to some extent, identify everyone using its platform (assuming that the registered users are giving correct information about themselves). However, the platform does not collect personal information from its users on a decentralized crypto exchange (DEX). A DEX is a decentralized cryptocurrencies exchange in which trades are made between users without a third-party trust or intermediary. A DEX is equivalent to using a public pay phone. The payphone has no log or audit information about the person using it, and if you put a quarter into the phone, it has no way to trace back the owner of the funds. It's merely a public service that does not contain any personal information about the use of its service.

Therefore, these platforms cannot divulge anything about the people using them to execute transactions.

BLOCKCHAIN SECURITY: 51% ATTACKS

The main concern of most blockchains is preventing a 51% attack. A 51% attack may occur if a person or group works together to corrupt, undermine, or destroy a blockchain by disrupting its operations. For a 51% attack to succeed, the people attacking the blockchain must control 51% or more of the network's full nodes.

It is increasingly improbable that an active blockchain with many users will fall to a 51% attack. It is doubtful because a 51% attack is costly to launch, coordinate, and execute. Furthermore, acquiring the full nodes will require the hacker to purchase expensive computing equipment, stake native tokens for some time, and behave accordingly to gain access to the full node. Once the hacker has access to the full node, they must simultaneously attack the network and spread their malicious conduct. Furthermore, the attack must come from different blockchain regions, not just one section or area. Plus, the watchdogs, who look for suspicious or malicious conduct, would have to be a part of this plan. If the watchdogs are not part of the plan, at least one of them will likely realize something is wrong and alert the network operators. Such heightened alertness within the group of network operators would terminate any chance of a 51% attack being successful.

Then there are the full node operators who are not part of the 51% attack. They may realize something is amiss and alert the watchdogs and other operators to understand what's happening on the network. And this, too, would terminate a 51% attack.

The final reason why a 51% attack is unlikely is that it would come at a high personal cost to anyone invested in the network or who has purchased the network's native tokens. Besides paying for the equipment to operate full nodes, staking crypto tokens to manage the nodes and bribing people to look the other way during the attack would mean the attackers would be losing all the money they invested in that network.

For blockchains like Ethereum and Bitcoin, the cost of a 51% attack would be astronomical. Furthermore, if the watchdogs or node operators capture the hackers, the penalty would most likely be losing any stake in cryptocurrencies and being banned from the network.

In addition, the crypto community will ban the hacker and make him unable to participate in other blockchain projects.

CONSENSUS ALGORITHMS

A consensus algorithm is a protocol a blockchain uses to check information on its transactions and ensure that all the data is correct.

For example, under the Proof of Work, or PoW, consensus algorithm used for mining cryptocurrency (e.g., Bitcoin, Ethereum), miners competed to solve complex mathematical equations to win the right to mine a block. The miners use energy-guzzling computers with high computational abilities to guess the answers to complex mathematical equations. As miners submit their incorrect guesses to the network, other miners use those wrong guesses to improve their guesses to have a better chance of guessing the correct answer. The first miner to guess the correct answer would have already seen similar solutions or answers close to his. In this way, miners check each other's work.

After a miner guesses the correct answer, the miner puts the transactions in a block and cements them into the blockchain. Note, while a miner is constructing a block, other miners compete to mine the next block. When miners complete a block, and the block is ready to be added to the blockchain, the miner does not simply add it to the next block. Instead, the miner who has won the right to add a block to the just-completed block will have to participate in the minting process of the finished block before miners can add his block to it. Minting is a form of checks and balances. No one miner can mint an entire block by himself. Cooperation between the miners and other people checking the information on the block and the transaction confirmations before the blocks are sealed and added to the next block.

If there are any block problems, miners will report the problems to another network operator so that operators can investigate them. Why? Because if miners find a problem with the minted blocks or how the miners process the block, the blockchain rewards the miners with native tokens for being vigilant and protecting the blockchain.

TRANSACTION SPEED

Transaction speed refers to the rate at which a blockchain can process and confirm the transactions executed on it. The term transactions per second (TPS) refers to the transaction speed of a blockchain. Blockchains with a high TPS rate can simultaneously service many people and are less likely to become congested during high traffic. They are also more likely to have low transaction fees. As their TPS gets higher and higher, they become more akin to traditional financial systems like those operated by Visa and Mastercard.

Let's look at some numbers.

Cryptocurrency	Transactions Per Second (TPS)	Average Transaction (Block) Confirmation Time
Bitcoin	3-7	10 min
Ethereum	15-25	6 min
Solana	2,825	0.4 sec
Polkadot	1,000	4-5 sec
EOS	4,000	0.5 sec
Cosmos	10,000	2-3 min
Stellar	1,000	2-5 sec
Dogecoin	30	1 min
Litecoin	56	30 min
Avalanche	5,000	1-2 sec
Algorand	1,000	45 sec
Ripple (XRP)	1,500	4 sec
Bitcoin Cash	61	60 min
IOTA	1,500	1-5 min
Dash	10-28	15 min

THE BLOCKCHAIN CHALLENGE: DECENTRALIZATION AND HIGH TPS RATE

For blockchains to become a part of everyday life and integrated into the existing financial system, they must significantly increase their TPS rate. Higher TPS rates are associated with efficiency, reliability, and scalability. To the point, blockchains must be scalable if they are going to be able to handle large numbers of transactions. Moreover, they must maintain their efficiency rates even when there's a large volume of traffic on the blockchain. The challenge for blockchain is to remain decentralized and still be secure, scalable, and efficient.

Let's compare centralized operations to the blockchain. Like Visa and Mastercard, centralized operations have servers, security personnel, and other support staff at one or more primary locations. This concentration of manpower and computing power enables the companies to securely, safely, and efficiently process more than a thousand transactions per second.

Unfortunately, this does not work for decentralized operations because there is a trade-off at some point. If a function is decentralized but lacks security and is not scalable, then at some point, it becomes an inefficient, unsafe database that will fail and/or be vulnerable.

NO DOUBLE-SPENDING

Double-spending occurs when a network user simultaneously tries to send the same crypto payment to two different addresses. For example, if you have only 5 BTC in your crypto wallet and try to send the 5 BTC to two other crypto wallets, you are trying to double-spend. Your two transactions will go into the mempool, where all submitted transactions reside until node operators select them. When miners choose your transactions, miners will process only one. The second one pulled will be rejected as invalid because you have no BTC in your crypto wallet (you used up all of your BTC in the first approved transaction).

If your transactions are selected simultaneously, the transaction that receives the most confirmations executes the consensus algorithm under the blockchain. The other transaction will be rejected, declared invalid, and discarded.

GOVERNANCE

Blockchains have a governance system to introduce or modify the blockchain's functionality. Governance refers to the way decisions are made about the blockchain's operations. Usually, decisions are made by those who can vote on proposals submitted to the system operations managers. Voters can vote for anyone who holds native tokens, those who own specific kinds of tokens (e.g., governance tokens), those with a particular amount/value of coins, and even investors in the blockchain. Still, the voters can restrict proposed changes to the blockchain. For example, for changes to the Ripple blockchain, at least 80% of its node operators must approve the change. If less than 80%

of its node operators agree on the transition to the blockchain, the operators reject the change.

BLOCKCHAIN FORKS: HARD & SOFT FORKS

We have discussed how blockchains work, how they maintain their trustworthiness, and how they process transactions. This section looks at what happens when the blockchain community members cannot agree on improving a blockchain.

When members of a blockchain community disagree on improving a blockchain, the situation may become very contentious. If the disagreement becomes polarizing, opposing factions can become deeply embedded in their position and resistant to compromise. However, members must reach a compromise if the in-fighting starts to tear the community apart. In these cases, we see the creation of hard forks and soft forks.

In-Fighting Gone Awry

If Group A of the blockchain community wants the blockchain to have more giant blocks so that the blocks can hold more transactions, but Group B wants the block size to stay the same, there will be a problem. If the groups cannot come to a compromise with each other, one of them may decide to launch another blockchain.

Launching another blockchain is not a win for the blockchain community because the more significant the blockchain community, the higher its market value, the more secure its network, and the more relevant it is in the crypto world. Therefore, when blockchains fork, generally, one of the two spectacularly fails or is overshadowed by the more successful blockchain. In addition, the original size of the blockchain community diminishes, and there's a decrease in the original blockchain's security. Forking success depends on how many community members stay with the original blockchain or migrate to the fork. Ultimately, the success of the division and the original blockchain rely on the network users and their respective communities.

Hard Forks

When there is a hard fork, transactions cannot process on the original blockchain on the fork and vice versa. The incompatibility is because the creators of the division substantively change the blockchain fork's code, so the separation is no longer compatible with the original blockchain. They then give the blockchain a new name and create a new native token (e.g., Bitcoin XT, Bitcoin Classic, Bitcoin Cash, Bitcoin Unlimited, Bitcoin Gold).

Soft Forks

When blockchain community members want options, they create a soft fork, but adding the options does not require them to abandon the original blockchain. In this case, the network users can use or ignore the additional feature. Soft forks do not get new names or have their own native tokens.

An example of a soft fork is the Segregated Witness (SegWit) protocol added to the Bitcoin blockchain. SegWit allowed users to add more transactions to a block by decreasing the data carried inside the block for each transaction. However, the change in block size allocation divided the Bitcoin community on whether to make it a permanent feature of the blockchain. The compromise was to make it an option that Bitcoin users could implement when setting up their transactions.

· · ·

Example: Hard Fork vs. Soft Fork

Using real-world examples, let's look at examples of a hard fork versus a soft fork.

Hard Fork

The original blockchain is like a road that runs alongside a river. Part of the blockchain community wants the blockchain to cross the river, but they are in the minority. The majority of the blockchain community wants blockchain transactions processed on the road. The people who wish for the blockchain to cross the river decide to launch the blockchain. Their network uses riverboats to process the transactions, whereas the original blockchain uses trucks on the road to process its transactions. Because these two forms of transportation are incompatible, the fork must have a completely different code from the original blockchain. Because the fork's programming is so other than the programming of the original blockchain, the two are incompatible. As a result, the original blockchain cannot execute the transactions intended for the fork, and the fork cannot process the transactions designed for the original blockchain. Therefore, the division must have a new name and its own native token.

Soft Fork

There are lots of streets going through every neighborhood in a city. These streets represent how the blockchain executes transactions. Group A in the blockchain community wants to build an overpass that bypasses the roads to process transactions faster. In addition, when there is heavy traffic on the streets, the overpass will help ease the congestion and prevent the transaction fees from becoming high. However, other people in the blockchain community disagree with the overpass idea and do not want it to become part of the blockchain. So, group A reaches a compromise with the other members of the community. It will design an overpass that community members can use for their transactions if they choose to use it. However, members will process their transactions if they do not want to use them.

In this case, the soft fork is compatible with the original blockchain. Blockchain users who want to use the overpass can use the network as usual but opt to take the overpass to avoid the congested city streets. Users who prefer the crowded city streets or don't want to use the overpass can simply elect not to have their transactions processed that way. In the case of a soft fork, there are no substantive changes to the blockchain code. Therefore, it does not get a new name or develop its own native token because it remains a part of the original blockchain.

COMMUNICATING BETWEEN DIFFERENT BLOCKCHAINS

Ethereum

Ethereum is the most versatile network in the crypto world. It hosts smart contracts, decentralized applications (dApps), other blockchains' tokens, non-fungible tokens (NFTs), and decentralized financial (DeFi) transactions.

To accentuate the attractiveness and usefulness of later launched blockchains (i.e., blockchains launched after Ethereum achieved prominence), many made themselves Ethereum-compatible. That means that the Ethereum-compatible blockchains' users could run their dApps and use their native tokens on the Ethereum blockchain, as well as access other services on it. Users like this option, because often, newer blockchains have faster TPS rates and lower transaction fees than the Ethereum blockchain, and with this option, they can still access all the services provided by the Ethereum blockchain.

For example, if someone created a dApp and wanted to move it to the Ethereum blockchain, it could be done with no problem and vice versa. Moreover, if someone started a blockchain game and wanted it to be available to people on the Ethereum blockchain and other Ethereum-compatible blockchains, it would be possible without changing the game's code.

The best part about Ethereum-compatible blockchains is that they can work with Ethereum when executing smart contracts and DeFi transactions. At this time, you can have a smart contract that exists on two different blockchains. As long as you use Ethereum and an Ethereum-compatible blockchain, the smart contract will work uniformly well on either blockchain. This is also increasingly true for DeFi transactions, which means that people will be able to take advantage of more DeFi apps—not just those hosted by their blockchain.

Polkadot

Polkadot is a blockchain that allows incompatible blockchains to communicate with one another. Using Polkadot, incompatible blockchains—like Bitcoin and Ethereum—can send value and data between one another. Polkadot's native token is DOT. Besides being used as a governance token and for staking, it can be used as a payment medium to transfer value from one blockchain to another.

Another benefit of using Polkadot is that it has a high TPS rate, is scalable, and uses parallel blockchains (parachains) to reduce the congestion on its network and maintain its high TPS rate. It retains its high TPS rate by having the parachains process most transactions.

Polkadot's main relay chain is its main blockchain that connects to the parachains. They process transactions, receive the confirmations, and then send the information to the main relay chain. The main relay chain checks the data from the parachains; if everything checks out, it adds the parachain's block to its blockchain.

Note that the parachains work within the Polkadot blockchain; they are not independent of it. Also, they are application-specific blockchains. Still, they are full blockchains with their consensus algorithms and security features as application-specific blockchains.

CHAPTER 4
THE ROADMAP TO CRYPTOCURRENCY OWNERSHIP

TAKE-HOME **Message**

The two types of crypto exchanges are centralized crypto exchanges (CEXs) and decentralized crypto exchanges (DEXs), and you should know about both. There are also several types of crypto wallets, and there may be one that is the best fit for you. After you set up a crypto account and purchase your first cryptocurrency, you can begin making decisions about which exchanges and wallets best fit your investment strategy.

WHAT IS A CRYPTOCURRENCY EXCHANGE?

A centralized crypto exchange is a digital marketplace where crypto tokens can be purchased, sold, and traded. Some popular centralized crypto exchanges (CEXs) are Coinbase, Kraken, Gemini, and Binance. These exchanges let their users purchase using fiat currency (cash) and cash out their cryptocurrencies to their bank accounts. However, not all CEXs allow their users to buy crypto tokens with fiat currency. On some CEXs, users can only buy, sell, and trade crypto tokens using other crypto tokens as a medium of exchange.

When buying, selling, and trading crypto tokens, platform users should look at the crypto pairing on the CEX. First, they should note if a crypto pairing exists. If the CEX does not list the crypto tokens the crypto holder wants to work with, the crypto holder should look for a different CEX for the transaction. Crypto tokens can only be bought, sold, and traded if listed on a CEX. The listing on the CEX means that the CEX has approved the crypto tokens for its platform and will allow users to use them in different transactions. In addition, when crypto tokens are listed, they are often paired with other crypto tokens, so platform users know the exchange rates between additional crypto tokens.

In short, crypto pairings are the exchange rates used between two different crypto tokens. So, for example, if you wanted to buy Litecoin using Bitcoin, you would go to a CEX that has Litecoin and Bitcoin as a crypto pairing. Then, after looking at the crypto pairing and the exchange rate, you would decide if you wanted to exchange your Bitcoin for Litecoin on that CEX.

SELECTING THE BEST CENTRALIZED CRYPTO EXCHANGE FOR YOU

All centralized CEXs do not offer the same services to their users. Therefore, crypto holders should investigate each CEX they are considering using for their crypto transactions.

Let's look at some factors crypto holders should consider when evaluating CEXs for their crypto transactions.

ACCESSIBILITY

You will want to be able to access your CEX easily. For example, China has banned all crypto exchanges from operating within its borders. In other places, like the US, crypto exchanges may be prohibited in certain parts of the country (e.g., New York state).

SECURITY

Because the Federal Deposit Insurance Corporation (FDIC) does not federally insure your crypto tokens like a US bank account, you'll want to use a CEX that is very secure.

When checking out potential CEXs, you want to look at how recently and how often each CEX has been hacked or lost funds due to fraudulent conduct. Also, you should check social media forums (e.g., Reddit, Discord, Twitter) for complaints by platform users about CEXs' security and the scams operating on their platforms.

INSURANCE

Another consideration is whether the CEX insures the crypto assets of its users. For example, some CEXs, like Coinbase, offer crypto holders insurance against hacking. For instance, if hackers hack Coinbase and steal crypto assets, Coinbase has an insurance policy that covers up to US$255 million for its combined user base on the platform. In this case, even if Coinbase's platform is hacked, if the value of the tokens stolen does not exceed US$255 million, crypto holders on the platform will not lose any of their assets.

STORAGE

Now, let's look at crypto storage practices—specifically, what percentage of the crypto assets are kept offline in cold storage. The more significant the portion of crypto assets held in cold storage, the harder it is for hackers to steal them. For example, Coinbase only keeps 2% of its crypto assets online. The assets that it does save online are the ones actively traded. The remainder, 98%, are kept in cold storage and backed by Coinbase's insurance policy.

TWO-FACTOR AUTHENTICATION

You can increase the security of your crypto account by activating a two-factor authentication code on your account. In addition to using your username and password to access your crypto account on a CEX, you must also enter a code sent to your mobile phone or email address. This code is additional proof/confirmation that you are authorized to access the account. This extra security feature may help prevent your crypto from being stolen by someone who has accessed your username and password.

LARGER VS. SMALLER CRYPTOCURRENCY EXCHANGES

There are differences between small CEXs and larger CEXs. The larger a CEX, the less likely it is to be hacked. Larger CEXs have larger trading volumes, higher levels of security, and, most likely, more personnel working to keep the platform secure than smaller CEXs. On the other hand, smaller CEXs with lower trading volume, and consequently less money, often do not have the same level of security as large CEXs, and their protocols are not updated as frequently.

In addition, some larger CEXs, like Coinbase, are now listed on stock exchanges (e.g., NASDAQ) and have been approved by governmental agencies. These CEOs are more credible and trustworthy because they:

- have been able to meet the regulatory standards of US governmental agencies;
- have been independently audited;
- maintain documentation on their operations;
- have established security protocols; and
- report on their operations regularly to the US government.

On the other hand, smaller CEXs often lack documentation, approval, and licenses from governmental agencies. As a result, smaller CEXs secure themselves with robust and comprehensive security protocols and build production management teams that closely watch their operations.

EXCHANGE FEES

Before selecting a CEX, review all the fees associated with using the CEX. Some CEXs have fixed transaction fees, but often the costs are a percentage of the crypto transaction itself. Other CEXs may charge fees based on the market price volatility. Of course, the fees may differ based on whether you are the buyer or the seller. In addition, they can vary depending on which crypto tokens you trade on the platform.

Note, the higher the fees on a CEX, the more likely it is that the CEX is secure and easy to conduct transactions on. Conversely, the lower the prices are on CEX, the less likely you will receive support from it. In addition, you are more likely to have some difficulty conducting transactions on it as a beginning crypto investor.

If you have never used a CEX before, you may be unfamiliar with the fees CEXs may charge their users. For example, payment services company may charge fees for making deposits or withdrawals, redeeming crypto tokens, and trading crypto tokens. They may also set prices based on depositing fiat currency into your account. For example, credit card companies charge the highest fees if you use a credit/debit card to purchase cryptocurrencies. Banks charge wire transfer fees between bank accounts too. On the other hand, some CEXs, like Binance, do not charge fees for deposits and withdrawals.

Best Crypto Exchanges and Apps

Broker	NerdWallet rating ⓘ	Fees	Account minimum
GEMINI Gemini	★ 5.0 /5 Best for Crypto exchanges	0.5% - 3.99% depending on payment method and platform	$0
eToro eToro	★ 4.0 /5 Best for Crypto exchanges	1% for cryptocurrency	$10
kraken Kraken	★ 5.0 /5 Best for Crypto exchanges	0.9%-2% varies by type of transaction; other fees may apply	$0
crypto.com Crypto.com	★ 4.5 /5 Best for Crypto exchanges	0%-2.99% varies by type of transaction; other fees may apply	$0
BINANCE Binance.US	★ 4.5 /5 Best for Crypto exchanges	0.1%-5% depending on payment method	$10

Image from "11 Best Crypto Exchanges and Apps of August 2022." [2]

LIQUIDITY

Check the liquidity and trading volume of the CEX. The higher the trading volume, the higher its liquidity. Liquidity is essential to you because when you want to sell, buy, or trade crypto tokens, an exchange with a high trading volume will let you do this easily. In comparison, an exchange with low trading volume may not be able to facilitate your crypto trading at preferred prices. Consequently, the delay in purchasing or selling your tokens on CEXs with low trading volumes may cause you to buy and sell at prices that decrease your potential profits.

LISTED TOKENS

CEXs are where you can buy, sell, and trade crypto tokens. They also list crypto pairings. You can trade cryptocurrencies with different crypto pairings listed on a CEX. Not every CEX lists every crypto on the market. The point is to find a CEX with the cryptocurrencies you want to purchase or trade while finding both the lowest purchase and transaction fees. When selecting a CEX, make sure it lists the tokens you are interested in trading, selling, and buying. Some popular crypto pairings are:

- ETH and Bitcoin Cash (BCH)
- BTC and Litecoin (LTC)
- BTC and USD Tether (USDT)
- BCH and USDT

EDUCATIONAL TOOLS

CEXs may offer educational tools that help its users learn about the crypto marketplace and stay up-to-date. These tools can include videos, quizzes, articles, and courses. Sometimes, you can earn crypto tokens by completing educational activities on the platform (e.g., quizzes).

TAX INFORMATION

Some CEXs provide their platform users with tax statements (e.g., 1099-B). These statements can be used by users to file their taxes correctly. However, most traditional CEXs (e.g., Coinbase, Kraken, Binance) only log transactions and do not provide tax statements. They do not offer tax statements because they cannot track your crypto transactions after you leave their platforms. In addition, they do not track your crypto assets after you transfer them to your private (i.e., off-CEX) crypto wallet.

DECENTRALIZED CRYPTO EXCHANGES

Decentralized crypto exchanges (DEXs) are digital marketplaces where crypto holders can buy, sell, and trade crypto tokens. They differ from CEXs in that users don't have to register an account with DEXs, and DEXs do not take custody of their crypto tokens during crypto transactions. Some popular DEXs are Uniswap, PancakeSwap, and SushiSwap.

DEXs are terrific for people who want to maximize their financial privacy with almost no oversight. Plus, they have other services that attract users to their platforms. Such services include automated market makers (to help you trade crypto tokens) and crypto wallet extensions that optimize token prices and decrease swap and slippage fees.

DEXs can be especially useful because they often carry newly launched tokens that do not have high trading volumes, tokens of low value that have low trading volumes, and highly speculative and risky tokens. These tokens are not likely to be listed on CEXs because CEXs have requirements that must be met before tokens can be listed on the platform. Unfortunately, most newly launched tokens, low-value tokens, and highly speculative tokens do not satisfy the listing requirements of CEXs. Tokens that do not meet the criteria of CEXs instead often list on DEXs.

Token Options

DEXs can list any token hosted by its blockchain. Therefore, they have access to newly launched tokens before they list on CEXs. But unfortunately, they also list a lot of scam tokens. Thus, platform users must be careful when trading tokens on a DEX.

Anonymity

There is no account registration process, know your customer (KYC) protocol, or anti-money-laundering (AML) protocol on DEXs. Instead, DEX users engage in private P2P transactions using smart contracts. The DEXs do not identify contracting parties or store personal information on their platforms. Consequently, for crypto holders who want absolute anonymity, DEXs are the best crypto exchanges.

Reduced Risk of Hacking

Platform users are less likely to have their crypto token stolen during a transaction on a DEX. Crypto holders maintain custody of their crypto assets on a DEX until they transfer them to another crypto wallet. At no time do DEXs take control or possess their platform users' crypto assets.

Reduced Transaction Risks

DEX contracts on the blockchain are the way of smart contracts. If the two contracting parties fulfill their obligations, the transaction completes. If they do not fulfill their responsibilities, the agreement expires. Smart contracts do not allow for partial completion of the contract. Therefore, on DEXs, there is a reduced risk of contract problems if there is inappropriate conduct by either party to the agreement.

EVERYTHING YOU WANTED TO KNOW ABOUT CRYPTO WALLETS

WHAT IS A CRYPTO WALLET?

Crypto wallets, also known as blockchain wallets, are places where you store your crypto tokens and NFTs. They are helpful for the following activities:

- Storing cryptocurrency
- Selling, buying, and trading cryptocurrency
- Selling, buying, and trading NFTs
- Trading on crypto exchanges

CRYPTO WALLET PASSWORDS AND SECRET SEED PHRASES

You are in control of your crypto wallet. It is like a decentralized bank account that you can use for digital transactions. But, also necessary, you must remember your crypto wallet password and secret seed phrase. The password opens the crypto wallet and gives you access to the crypto tokens and NFTs stored. The private seed phrase allows you to recover your crypto wallet if you forget your password.

Your secret seed phrase will have 12 to 24 words in it. The words are common words found in an English dictionary. However, the words must be entered into your crypto wallet app in a particular order if you want to recover your crypto wallet. An example of a secret seed phrase is "witch collapse practice feed shame open despair creek road again ice least." If you forget your password and lose your secret seed phrase, you lose access to your crypto wallet and everything in it.

You must keep your wallet password and secret seed phrase private. You must never tell anyone your wallet password or secret seed phrase. Secret seed phrase confidentiality is necessary because any person can access your crypto assets with either of these pieces of information.

CUSTODIAL VS. NON-CUSTODIAL WALLETS

A crypto wallet maintained on a CEX (e.g., Robinhood, Kraken, Binance, Coinbase) is a custodial wallet. CEXs are operated by a central authority, just like a bank. The central authority can take possession of your assets, deny withdrawals or receipts of cryptocurrencies to your custodial wallet, or even remove you from the platform.

Non-custodial wallets are independent private crypto wallets. Some examples of non-custodial wallets are Trezor, Ledger Nano X, Exodus, Coinbase Wallet, Mycelium, and Electrum. These wallets can be specialized to deliver optimal performance in different situations. For example, some crypto wallets are excellent for cell phones and desktops. Other wallet designs are good for beginning crypto investors, DeFi investors, or investors who want to invest in NFTs.

PRIVATE KEYS

The blockchain uses private keys to grant access to your cryptocurrency balance on the blockchain and permit transactions. In addition, private keys determine the owner because only the owner can transfer the cryptocurrency to other crypto accounts and use it in transactions. In real-world terms, private keys are similar to the PIN of a credit or debit card. If you give someone your PIN, that person can use your PIN to remove money from your credit or debit account.

Private keys should be kept secure. For example, you may want to use a USB drive with a password to store your private keys. In addition, you should back up any information stored on that USB, because if you lose your private keys, you lose your crypto . . . forever.

PUBLIC KEYS

Crypto wallets have public keys, also known as public addresses. The public keys are composed of a string of random letters and numbers to identify crypto wallets. The public key is like a bank account number that you can freely share with others. You use a public key as a destination address in crypto transactions. As a real-world analogy, the public key of a crypto wallet is like a bank account number. People with your bank account number can send you money without your other personal details.

PUBLIC-PRIVATE KEY ENCRYPTION

When a network issues a crypto token, the token has a private key. The private key generates a public key linked to the private key cryptographically. You can give anyone your public key, but you must never give anyone your private key.

Public keys are generated from private keys using a process called hashing. Hashing processes a string of data using an algorithm. The method of creating the public key is almost impossible to reverse engineer. So, it is highly improbable that anyone can guess or deduce your private key from your public key. As a result, these encrypted keys keep your crypto assets safe and secure.

People can send you crypto tokens that are compatible with your crypto wallet using your wallet's public key (i.e., public address). So, if your crypto wallet is Ethereum-compatible, you can receive Ethereum-compatible crypto tokens. However, you must have the wallet's password to access the crypto tokens in your wallet. As a real-world analogy, your wallet's public key is like a bank account number. Likewise, the wallet's password is like the PIN of your credit or debit card.

SINGLE VS. MULTI-CHAIN WALLETS

There are two types of crypto wallets: single-chain and multi-chain wallets. The kind of wallet a person decides to use will depend on the interactions the person wants to have with a blockchain or blockchains.

Single-Chain Wallet

. . .

Single-chain wallets are wallets that you use for one public blockchain. This kind of wallet is most beneficial to people with an elevated level of commitment or a professional need to maintain a close connection with a specific public blockchain. For example, the people who would use a single-chain wallets are traders, miners, and dApp developers who prefer to use a particular public blockchain. If someone has a single-chain crypto wallet, the crypto wallet only has one public address or one public key because it is used with one public blockchain.

Multi-Chain Wallet

Multi-chain wallets allow their owners to store digital assets from multiple public blockchains in their crypto wallets. For example, a multi-chain wallet can store Bitcoin, Ether, EOS, and DOT. Crypto holders would have to hold numerous single-chain wallets on their electronic devices (e.g., mobile phone, desktop, laptop, tablet) to use single-chain wallets for different blockchains. However, with a multi-chain wallet, only one wallet needs to be installed on an electronic device for the crypto holder to access multiple public blockchains.

CRYPTO WALLET ADDRESSES

Your multi-chain crypto wallet will have a unique address for each different type of cryptocurrency stored in it. In short, your multi-chain crypto wallet will have separate addresses for your Ether, Bitcoin, and DOT tokens.

When you want to receive crypto tokens from different blockchains, you need only copy the 25- to 30-character string address and paste it into the transaction box. These addresses enable you to receive cryptocurrency from other accounts.

TYPES OF CRYPTO WALLETS

There are two main categories of crypto wallets: hot and cold. A hot wallet (e.g., web wallet, desktop wallet) is a software wallet connected to the internet. On the other hand, a cold wallet (e.g., hardware, paper) does not connect to the internet.

Hot Wallets

If your wallet is online, it is called a hot wallet. Because hot wallets are constantly accessible online, they are less secure than cold wallets. In addition, they are less secure because access to a hot wallet is continuously available.

Their attractiveness comes from their ease of use, convenience, and suitability for daily trading. Hot wallets are easy to set up, their funds are easily accessed, and they are readily available for traders and crypto investors.

Cold Wallets

Cold wallets are crypto wallets that do not connect to the internet. These wallets are hack-proof because hackers cannot access them. These wallets are perfect for HODLers (i.e., people who only hold crypto) and those who do not trade daily. However, you must connect the wallet to the internet to use the crypto stored in a cold wallet. Therefore, crypto investors must ensure that they use a secure connection when connecting their cold wallets to the internet. If crypto traders do not secure their links, hackers may hack their links amid a transaction and steal crypto assets.

Hardware Wallets

A hardware wallet is a device you can connect to your desktop or laptop and store your public and private keys on. It looks like a USB. It has no battery and can access all your desktop apps.

These wallets are more secure than hot wallets but less user-friendly than paper wallets. You can find a variety of them on the market at different prices. Often, beginning crypto investors find them challenging to use. Some examples of hardware wallets are Ledger Nano S and Trezor.

Paper Wallets

Paper wallets are the least popular crypto wallets because they require strict security precautions. Also, generally, paper wallets can only be used once. Plus, you cannot send partial funds via a paper wallet.

They are hack-proof because they do not connect to the internet. To use these wallets, you must download a printed QR code. Although some paper wallets allow users to download a code and generate new addresses offline, others do not. Before investing in a paper wallet, you should research its cost, recommended security precautions, and how many transactions you can perform with your paper wallet.

Desktop Wallets

· · ·

Desktop wallets are wallets you install on your desktop or laptop. You must install the anti-virus software that comes with these wallets. The anti-virus software is essential because it will prevent your crypto transactions from being hacked when accessing your wallet or connecting it to a blockchain. These wallets are user-friendly, don't use third parties, provide anonymity, and give you privacy. Some desktop wallets are Exodus, Bitcoin Core, and Electrum.

Mobile Wallets

Mobile wallets are like desktop wallets, but the wallet's design is optimal for mobile phone performance. Unfortunately, despite being well-designed for daily transactions, they are vulnerable to infection by malware. These wallets must also be encrypted so that anyone hacking your mobile phone cannot easily access your crypto wallets or transactions. If you are interested in mobile wallets, check out Coinomi and Mycelium.

Web Wallets

Web wallets are accessed using Internet browsers and are vulnerable to many online attacks (e.g., phishing, malware, browser extension risks). They may be hosted or non-hosted online. Hosted ones are more likely to be hacked than non-hosted ones. It is better to use non-hosted wallets because you are always directly controlling your funds with them. They are suitable for small investments and NFTs. Some examples of web wallets are MetaMask and Coinbase.

CREATING AN ACCOUNT ON A CENTRALIZED CRYPTOCURRENCY EXCHANGE

Are you ready to open a CEX account? If you haven't opened one yet, this tutorial can help you do it. This tutorial teaches you how to open a CEX account on Coinbase. The process is similar when you open accounts on other CEXs.

Before creating your CEX account, review the following checklist. When you can answer "yes" to all the questions on the list, you are ready to open your Coinbase account.

Checklist:

- Are you 18 years of age or older?
- Do you have government-issued identification (e.g., a driver's license or passport)?
- Do you have a computer or mobile phone that is connected to the Internet?
- Do you have a phone number connected to your mobile phone? (You need one to receive Coinbase's SMS messages.)
- Are you using the most up-to-date version of your Internet browser?

You are now ready to open your Coinbase account.

Setting Up Your Coinbase Account
Section I

1. Go to https://www.coinbase.com or download the app to your mobile phone.
2. Click on the "Create free account" button (mobile) or

"Sign Up" button (desktop). On desktop, choose the account type "Individual."

3. Enter the following information on the page:
4. Full Legal Name (the one listed on your government identification)
5. Email Address
6. Password (keep a copy of it somewhere safe and secure)
7. Review the User Agreement and Privacy Policy.
8. Check the box stating that you agree with both of them.
9. Click the "Create free account" button.

Section 2

1. Verify your email address when you receive an email request from Coinbase asking you to confirm your email address.
2. Click the link in the email. It will take you back to the Coinbase website.
3. Sign in to your account using your email address and password. (Use the same email address to which Coinbase sent the email confirmation request earlier.)
4. Add your phone number to your account when the website prompts you to.
5. Select the country to which your mobile phone number is registered (desktop).
6. Type in your mobile phone number.
7. Click the "Send code" button (desktop) or the "Continue" button (mobile).
8. Type in the 7-digit code sent by Coinbase (to your computer or mobile phone).

9. Double-click the "Submit" button (desktop) or the "Continue" button (mobile).
10. If you did not receive the 7-digit code, double-click the "Resend code" button.

Section 3

1. Choose the country of your citizenship.
2. Enter the following information from your government identification:
3. First Name
4. Last Name
5. Date of Birth
6. Last 4 Digits of your SSN
7. Address
8. Answer the following questions:
9. What will you primarily use Coinbase for?
10. What's your primary source of funds?
11. What's your employment status?
12. What's the total value – including cash and crypto – that you expect to transfer to your Coinbase account in the next 12 months?
13. What industry do you work in?

Section 4

1. Click "Add a payment method" to link a payment method to your account. For example, you can use your bank account, debit card, wire transfers, PayPal, Apple Pay, Google Pay, and instant cash outs to bank accounts in the US.

2. Click "Continue" when Coinbase prompts you to use Plaid to connect your account.
3. Select your institution.
4. Enter your credentials.
5. Verify your identity via text, phone, or email.
6. Select the bank account you wish to link to Coinbase.
7. Select "Continue."

Section 5

1. Sign in to your Coinbase account.
2. Go to "Profile & Settings" on your mobile phone or "Settings" on your desktop computer.
3. If you are on a mobile phone, go to "Require PIN / Face ID" and toggle the switch on. Enter a PIN you will remember. Choose the settings you would like for your PIN / Face ID.
4. If you are on a mobile phone, install one of the following apps: Google Authenticator, Duo Mobile, or Microsoft Authenticator.
5. Go to your Security Settings again. Click "Change security settings" and continue in browser.
6. Navigate to "2-step verification."
7. Click "Select" under the option to install an Authenticator app on your phone.
8. Enter the 2-step verification code sent to your mobile phone and click "Confirm."
9. Click the QR code to copy the app's seed to your phone's clipboard.
10. Open your Authenticator app.
11. Select the option to enter a key. For account name, type "Coinbase." Then click "paste" in the box for the key. This will generate a time-sensitive authentication code.

Navigate back to Coinbase and enter the code into the 2-step verification code from the authenticator app.

12. Click "Enable." You have now enabled two-step verification. This provides your Coinbase account with additional protection and security from unauthorized access.

Buying Your First Cryptocurrency

Using a Computer

1. Sign in to your Coinbase account.
2. Click on the "Buy & Sell" button in the upper-right corner of your screen.
3. Click the "Buy" button to select the crypto token you want to purchase.
4. Enter the amount of the selected crypto token you want to purchase in local currency or the selected crypto token currency.
5. Choose your payment method.
6. Click on "Preview Buy" to verify your purchase. If there is a problem with the purchase, click the "Back" button to edit your transaction.
7. If your transaction details are correct, click the "Buy" button to finish your purchase.
8. To make repeated purchases, like the one you have just completed, click the "One Time Purchase" button, and choose how often you want to repeat the purchase.
9. When you finish, sign out of your account.

Using the Coinbase Mobile App

1. Sign in to your Coinbase account.
2. Touch the "Buy" button on the "Home" tab.
3. Choose the crypto token you want to buy.
4. Enter the amount you want to buy in local currency or in the currency of the crypto token you wish to purchase.
5. Tap the "Preview Buy" button to check your transaction details.
6. Touch the "Buy Now" button if all the details are correct.
7. If you want to make repeated transactions like the one you just completed, tap the "One Time Purchase" button, and choose how frequently you want to make purchases.
8. When you finish, sign out of your account.

Note: The minimum purchase amount is 2.00, whether it's US$2.00 or EUR€2.00.

CHAPTER 5
CASE STUDY – WHOLESOME BOUNTY GARDENERS AND THE BLOCKCHAIN REVOLUTION

NOW LET'S put what we learned about the blockchain in perspective.

To better understand the blockchain, let's run through an example of a group of community gardeners that utilize a blockchain to assist in exchanging their garden's yield for their newly created cryptocurrency.

Liam was part of a local community garden group called the Wholesome Bounty Gardeners, which had over 40 members that grew and traded produce with each other. Liam was an avid learner of blockchain technology and wanted to leverage blockchain technology to facilitate transactions amongst the community gardeners. So, he created a blockchain for the community and called it the "WBG Blockchain," and the coin transacted on the WBG blockchain was known as "garden coin."

How can the blockchain help the Wholesome Bounty Gardeners?

. . .

Liam knew that the WBG community needed to store transaction data in a way that nobody could change the transaction data once the transaction occurred. He knew blockchain technology was the solution because there would be no way to hack and change the number of garden coins on the blockchain. Each transaction needed to reference an identifier in the previous transaction, creating a chain of transactions. This chain of transactions needed to be immutable once created, otherwise known as an *immutable ledger*. Liam did not want this immutable ledger running only on his computer, so he wrote the blockchain to run on multiple computers in the WBG group. Running the blockchain this way would, in turn, provide multiple copies of the immutable ledger and *decentralize* control of the blockchain amongst the members of the WBG. So, each computer with a copy of this transaction ledger would be considered a *node* on the blockchain. Liam wanted members of the WBG to transact with each other; also, he did not want to be involved in the transaction or have any authority over the transaction, otherwise knowns as *peer-to-peer transactions*.

How is it that Liam doesn't have authority over the transactions if all the WBG member accounts are on the blockchain?

Liam knew the basic design of the blockchain was *trustless*. But, first, he needed to show the community how the WBG blockchain had no third-party oversight. He indicated that the WBG blockchain privately generated keys when a member requested a private key to access the blockchain. The keys would come in pairs, a *receive* key and a *private key*. The receiver or *public* key would be a key that members would give out to their peers that wanted to send them garden coins. The private key was a key that each user would use to access the blockchain to view and send coins linked to their private key.

Example of what a private key looks like:
    8efe77fc4e66ad2ea7eaec900ed5c38733b569576f4a-
ca3042428b85811e0bc4

What if someone guessed the other members' private keys or the WBG blockchain created duplicate private keys?

Liam knew questions about the security of the WBG would come up, because a good deal of the WBG members' time and energy would be recorded digitally on the blockchain, and the community wanted some assurance of the integrity of the WBG blockchain. So first, Liam explained to the community that the blockchain's privately generated key had 2 to the 256 power (2^{256}) numbers in it—or a number with 77 digits of different possible combinations. So, guessing someone else's private key or ending up with duplicate private keys was virtually impossible. Liam went further to make a comparison below.[3]

- *There are an estimated 7.5×10^{18} grains of sand on Earth.*
- *There are estimations of anywhere from 30×10^{21} to 70×10^{21} and even 10×10^{23} stars in the "observable" universe.*
- *There is an estimation of anywhere from 1×10^{78} to 1×10^{83} atoms in the known, observable universe.*

So, there are more private key combinations than grains of sand, stars, and atoms in the universe combined. That's a whole lot of private key combinations, making it practically impossible to duplicate or guess.

. . .

So, guessing someone else's private was practically impossible, but what if someone lost their private key?

Liam realized that because the private key was impossible to recover if members lost it, he let the WBG community know of several ways to safeguard their private keys. First, he let the community know that in addition to the private key, there would be a 12-word secret *seed phrase* to generate the private key, and it would be much easier to remember the words in the seed phrase than the private key. Members could commit the seed phrase to memory to ensure they would not lose access to their garden coins on the WBG blockchain. Secondly, Liam recommended members also take the seed phrase and write it down or copy it to a USB drive and hide it in a safe location.

Now that WBG Members had their private keys, what were they to do with them?

Liam knew there had to be a portal that WBG members could connect to view and send their garden coin holdings. However, Liam did not want access to the gang's private keys in any way, so he set up a *non-custodial wallet* option for members to access their garden coins. Liam had several non-custodial wallet options for the community: *a web wallet, desktop, or mobile wallet*. The team would input their private keys into the wallet, and the wallet would then connect to the WBG blockchain, allowing members to view their garden coin holdings or send garden coins to other members. The wallet would also have the *receiving address* the members would give other members to receive garden coins.

· · ·

How does Liam's blockchain integrate with the Wholesome Bounty Gardeners community's fruits and vegetable yield?

So, let's say the community garden trades fruits and vegetables amongst one another. One of the participants didn't produce enough crops one year and wanted to exchange something other than vegetables with the rest of the group. So, if Oliver wanted three bags of potatoes from Sally, Oliver could now send to Sally's public receiver key three garden coins on Liam's newly written WBG blockchain.

But where did Oliver get his three garden coins?

Oliver decided to help build out the blockchain by running the blockchain program and investing in a desktop computer to run the blockchain node 24/7, not to mention the electricity required to keep the blockchain running continuously throughout the day. Each time someone in the community garden would make a transaction, Oliver's computer would work on solving a mathematical problem to link transactions on the blockchain. And as compensation for running a *node* in the WBG blockchain, Oliver would be awarded a newly minted garden coin; this process is better known as *Proof of Work*.

What if Oliver's or Liam's blockchain node went down? Or both went down?

One of the WBG members, Joel, asked, "What if Oliver's node goes down? Does that mean all our transactions are gone?" Liam knew that one of the critical features of blockchains is *persistence*, or no data loss. He knew that if the transaction ledger was lost, then the ownership of all the hard work and effort would also be forfeited. So, Liam told Joel and the WBG group that the blockchain algorithm also copied the transaction ledger onto Liam's blockchain node. So, there were two live copies of the transaction ledger. Then Joel asked, "What if both computers are down?" Liam said that no one could transact if both computers went down, but the transaction ledger would still be on the hard drive on both the computers, and once the computers came back up, the transaction ledger would be accurate. Then Joel's wife, Olivia, said, "Now wait a second. That's all good and fine that the blockchain replicated the transaction ledger on two computers. But what if Oliver's node is down, and Liam's is still running? Doesn't that mean the blockchain has missing transaction data when Oliver's computer comes back online?" The WBG group was quite shocked at Olivia's poignant question.

Liam knew quite well the importance of having the integrity of the data be consistent and update-to-date on the blockchain. So, Liam began to talk about the WBG blockchain's *consensus algorithm*. First, Liam explained to the group that the blockchain would compare the copies of the transaction ledger on all the nodes and use the transaction ledger with the greatest number of transactions in the chain. The blockchain algorithm would then replicate the longest transaction ledger to all the other nodes on the blockchain. Olivia then thought more about the consensus algorithm and realized that this would indeed keep the integrity of the transaction data.

Olivia, not completely satisfied, then interjected again about the integrity of the blockchain.

. . .

Olivia, with another inspirational thought, interjected again! She asked, "What if you and Oliver got together and secretly modified the transaction ledger?" With that thought alone, most of the WBG Blockchain gang gasped and began nodding their heads in agreement. Liam explained that the success and the trust in the blockchain happen by giving the community a way to view the ledger publicly, otherwise known as the *public ledger.* Liam also mentioned to the gang that not only would the transactions be able to be viewed publicly but the integrity of the transaction data would be even more robust if more members of the community had a blockchain node running in their houses. By having more nodes running, the WBG blockchain would have more copies of the transaction ledger on members' computers, and the less likely anyone would be to be able to modify the transaction registry on all the nodes all at once. Again, Olivia saw the merits of the public ledger and running more blockchain nodes. Her final response to Liam was, "Touché."

It's fine for Oliver to mint new garden coins, but what about the other WBG members?

Well, little did folks in the community garden know that Liam had been putting in 100 hours per week writing the blockchain for the community and didn't even have time to grow his vegetables. However, Liam needed help to write and maintain the blockchain and educate others on how the blockchain would benefit the community. So, Liam proposed something new and exciting: members who could help promote and support the blockchain would get newly minted garden coins. Blockchain builders of the community garden team could then trade their garden coins for fruits and veggies that the community grew.

. . .

So, aren't the blockchain builders of the community garden team now the third-party trust that blockchains are supposed to do away with?

No, because Liam decided to add several features unique to blockchains to allow for *fair governance*. First, *all* members have the ability to newly mint coins by supporting the blockchain, like how Oliver runs a node in his house to have a computer for the blockchain to run on. Secondly, Liam's blockchain has a governance system in which the more garden coins one has, the more votes that person has in the community on blockchain features and future enhancements.

In comes James, the mega grower in the community garden . . .

One of the community members was quite upset about the blockchain—at every level. He and his family of five generations knew the ins and out of making a productive garden. However, James didn't understand a thing about technology and didn't want to run a node. So, Liam and the garden community blockchain builders decided the way to help James was to build a marketplace in a member's backyard where veggies could be traded and stored. James then brought his 100 lbs. of veggies to the market, and in return, received 100 garden coins.

James was still upset; what could he do with 100 garden coins?

At the market, James thought Liam cheated him by only giving him 100 digital garden coins—basically invisible coins, he thought—while he had traded in his 100 lbs. of vegetables. So, after voicing his opinion at the market, Lucas the composter went to James and said, "I'll give you 100 lbs. of compost in exchange for your garden coins." James, an avid gardener, loved growing but didn't like the composting business because he wasn't fond of dealing with worms and rotting foods. So, James quickly agreed and made the transaction with Lucas. Lucas then used his garden coins at the market to buy fruits and veggies for his family and grandkids.

The blockchain solves problems for the Wholesome Bounty Gardeners.

In closing, we can see how the unique qualities of the blockchain can facilitate and assist in creating a store of value or wealth and exchange of this value peer-to-peer without a third-party trust profiting. We can see how the WBG Gardeners blockchain keeps evolving and expanding to fit the community's needs.

Disclaimer
The story in this chapter is a work of fiction. Names, characters, business, events, and incidents are the products of the author's imagination. Any resemblance to actual persons or events is purely coincidental. Any third-party trademarks mentioned herein are used solely for descriptive purposes and do not constitute or imply any sponsorship or endorsement of this material by such third parties unless expressly stated.

CHAPTER 6
BUILDING YOUR CRYPTOCURRENCY DEFENSES

TAKE-HOME **Message**

Crypto scams are increasing every year. You must be vigilant and take security precautions to make sure that you secure your crypto assets. There are numerous ways you can protect your crypto assets. Do the things that work best for you. Remember that once hackers steal your crypto, it's gone for good.

CRYPTOCURRENCY SCAMS ARE ON THE RISE

Cryptocurrency scams increase more than tenfold every year. The more money investors put into the crypto market, the more attractive it is to scammers and fraudsters.

People lose money every day in the crypto market. Unfortunately, new investors are susceptible to losing tons of money via scams, shoddy investments, and hacking. Crypto investors know that these scams and frauds exist to attract your interest and steal your crypto assets. Unfortunately, these scams are getting more attractive and persuasive and can look similar to legitimate offers and investments.

These scams are like the ones used with bank accounts and credit cards. The primary difference is that crypto scams use computer programming, Internet communication, and hacking skills. In addition, the perpetrators are hard to catch because cryptocurrency is borderless and can be accessed from anywhere in the world. So, good luck getting law enforcement to see them and get your crypto assets back.

This chapter will give you a brief overview of the most common crypto scams. Before we start, let me be blunt: There is no way to know whether a crypto token, blockchain, crypto exchange, or another type of crypto-related offering is entirely legitimate. The most you can do is look for signs that the advertised crypto or blockchain investment is what it claims to be.

FAKE CRYPTO EXCHANGES

The fake crypto exchanges offer services similar to legitimate crypto exchanges. The difference is that fraudulent exchanges target specific crypto tokens. The goal of the phony crypto exchange operators is to collect the private keys of as many crypto tokens as possible before they shut down the exchange and disappear.

You will realize there is a problem with the fraudulent exchange when you cannot move your crypto tokens to another address, redeem them, or exchange them for other crypto tokens. The operators of the fake crypto exchange will blame the problems on technology and then abscond with your crypto assets. Tragically, you and the other platform users will never recover your stolen crypto assets. Moreover, the fake crypto exchange operators will most likely never be found or forced to answer for their crimes.

Spotting Fake Crypto Exchanges

. . .

When you research the crypto exchange, ask yourself several questions. If you can't find satisfying answers to these questions, stay away from the crypto exchange.

The questions are:

- Can you find detailed information about the people operating the crypto exchange?
- Can you see the crypto exchange operators' social media accounts and profiles?
- Are the exchange operators' profiles and accounts active and up-to-date?
- Does the exchange have high liquidity?
- Is there enough capital invested in the crypto exchange to fund its growth, expansion, and maintenance?
- Does the crypto exchange have medium to high trading volume?
- Does the crypto exchange store your crypto tokens' private keys?
- Are you required to give the crypto exchange your personal information?
- Does the crypto exchange have a good reputation with other crypto enthusiasts?
- Are there any complaints about the crypto exchange's customer service?
- Is the crypto exchange being discussed on Twitter, Discord, or Reddit?
- Have crypto enthusiasts had any problems conducting crypto transactions on the crypto exchange?

HOW TO PROTECT YOURSELF

If you are not using a well-known CEX, transfer your crypto tokens out of your CEX account and into your private wallet regularly. Also, limit the information you give the CEX when registering your account. Note that some people have had their identities stolen using the information they provided to fake crypto exchanges to open their accounts. Finally, if an exchange is incredibly cheap and seems too good to be true, it is probably a phony crypto exchange.

FAKE CRYPTO WALLETS

Crypto investors can have their crypto tokens stolen by storing them in a fake crypto wallet. These wallets can be downloaded from the Internet or acquired from online shops. The problem is that these wallets are not legitimate software programs; they are created by scammers who want to steal your crypto assets. They usually have names similar to famous cryptocurrencies and crypto exchanges. They do this because they want to borrow the credibility of the established crypto company. They use a company's name, reputation, and market performance to get potential customers to trust and use their software.

Spotting a Fake Crypto Wallet

Before you choose a crypto wallet:

- Research the company.
- Check its performance history, customer complaint record, and social media forums for information about it.

- If you spot any red flags or questionable stuff, stay away from it.

HIDDEN WALLETS

Hidden wallets are crypto wallets in your computer or smartphone that have been put there by a hacker to steal your crypto. Deploying hidden wallets is done via the hacker getting access to your electronic device, creating a wallet on it, and giving the hidden wallet an address similar to your crypto wallet. The hacker will then go into your computer and locate places where you have copied your crypto wallet's address and change the address to the hidden wallet's address.

A hidden wallet scam works because people often copy their crypto wallet addresses and seldom check them (to ensure they are correct). So, when purchasing crypto tokens, they deposit them into the hidden wallet because they do not realize that the copied address is no longer the address of their crypto wallet. They only discover a problem when they check their crypto wallet's balance and recognize that the balance is incorrect.

Note that the victim cannot access the hidden wallet (e.g., withdraw the deposited tokens, spend the tokens in transactions) because only the hacker can access the contents of the hidden wallet.

PUMP-AND-DUMP SCHEMES

A group of people decides to make some quick profits from crypto. First, they all buy substantial amounts of a specific crypto token at a low market price. Then, after they have purchased their crypto tokens, they go to their social media accounts (e.g., Twitter, Discord, Reddit) and promote their recently purchased low-value crypto tokens as the next significant investment.

Scammers increase demand for the crypto token through false news that artificially increases market price. When the market price continues to rise, even more people will begin to pay attention to the crypto token and buy it. Over time, the token's price will continue to grow as it gets hotter and hotter. At some point, the pump-and-dump scheme organizers will slowly start selling off their tokens for a nice profit. Later, the scheme organizers will dump all of their holdings on the market. After they leave their coins, the market price of the tokens will sharply decline. As the price drops, the new investors will begin selling their cryptos because they fear losing their initial investment. Sadly, as more investors sell their holdings, the token price will drop even faster. As a result, the token price will likely return to its initial low market value or possibly drop even lower. The investors who bought the crypto token as its price rose will probably lose their initial investment.

Spotting a Pump-and-Dump Scheme

Before you start buying crypto tokens based on some tips you get from your social media forum or "friend," carefully research the crypto token. Treat the advice like it was information given to you by a random, suspicious-looking stranger at night while walking past him. In short, don't assume that everything you hear or read on a social media forum is true or backed by research. They are also great places to find dupes (AKA victims) for pump-and-dump schemes.

Ask yourself the following questions and get satisfying answers to them before you commit your resources to this potentially lucrative investment:

- Why is the crypto token in demand?
- Why is the crypto token's market price rising?
- Who is pushing the crypto token?

- Can you verify any of the information you received about the crypto token?
- After researching the crypto token, does it seem like a sound investment for you?

SHILLING SCAM

Crypto token holders spread false information about a token they are holding to increase the demand for it. They aim to increase the token's price to a level where they can sell their coins for a nice profit. The people duped into buying the cryptocurrency create the demand for it and are why its price increases over time. At some point, the shills will sell off their holdings (i.e., dump them on the market) and cause the token's market price to drop like a rock. The new investors will not realize the profits they anticipated or lose their initial investment. Because they were not part of the scam, they will not be beneficiaries of the scam's success.

Spotting a Shilling Scam

To prevent yourself from becoming a victim of a shilling scam, ask yourself several questions and get satisfying answers before you buy into a hot token that other people are pushing. The questions are:

- Who is providing the information about the cryptocurrency?
- Can you verify any of the information you have received about the token?
- Why would people want to own this crypto?
- Does the token's market history suggest that this current increase in its value is organic?

Because it can be challenging to answer these questions and get satisfying answers, just because you cannot answer them doesn't mean that the token is being shilled (e.g., Dogecoin). In such instances, you may have to take a leap of faith and hope it works out for you. But as always, never commit more capital to a questionable investment than you can comfortably avoid losing without regret.

PHISHING SCAMS

These scammers use emails and text messages to trick you into giving them access to your crypto assets. In the emails or text messages, they will try to get your personal information, crypto tokens' private keys, crypto wallet passwords, and other information that scammers can use to their advantage and detriment.

People generally send these by using official-looking emails or text messages. But unfortunately, they will also try to pressure you into immediately acting on the information by telling you that it is a limited-time offer or that it is limited to a small number of people on a first-come, first-served basis.

Spotting Phishing Scams

Before responding to a potential communication from a phishing scam, do the following:

- Research the company that is offering the deal, gifts, etc.
- Research the history of the offer and any offers similar to it.
- Know what kinds of information the communication is for and whether it could be used to steal your crypto assets or identity.

- Determine whether they are asking for personal information you would not give a nameless, faceless stranger.

Remember that nothing in life is free—not even Facebook!

CELEBRITY/INFLUENCER IMPERSONATORS

Be wary of any emails that you receive from supposed celebrities or influencers. Unless you are in contact with these people and their social circles, it is doubtful that they will send you a personal email to convince you to participate in a crypto give-away, contest, or hot crypto tip. You should have realized by now that the email message you received most likely came from someone impersonating a celebrity or influencer. These scammers expect you to be so impressed and excited by receiving an email from a famous or notable person that you would overlook the questionable aspects of the email, trust them, and give them what they want from you. For example, if you receive an email message from someone you admire but that you have never met, what are the chances that it was the person you admire who sent it to you?

Any unsolicited email or text message that gives you investment advice is sketchy. Treat it like advice from a random stranger with unknown intentions. When responding to such communications, do not give out personal information that can be used against you to steal your identity or assets (e.g., mother's maiden name, social security number).

Spotting Celebrity/Influencer Impersonator Communications

• • •

Before you respond to an unsolicited communication that invites you to participate in something you have never heard of and know nothing about, ask yourself the following questions:

- What is the goal of the communication?
- What does the sender of the communication want from you?
- What does the person who sent you the communication want you to do?
- What is your relationship with the person who sent the communication?
- How does the person know you?
- How trustworthy is the person who sent you the communication?
- How would you respond to the communication if it was sent to you by a random stranger you had never met, talked to, or heard of?

SIM HACK

Many crypto investors use their smartphones to perform crypto trades and transactions. They also check their crypto wallet balances, purchase crypto tokens, and perform other crypto-related tasks using smartphones.

Hackers who want to access their victims' crypto tokens or crypto wallets may do that by hacking their smartphones. Hackers only have to hack your SIM card one time. During that one-time hack, they can download viruses to your phone or even look through your files. Moreover, they can put code on your smartphone that lets hackers view activity on your phone, have information sent to them from your phone, and allows them to alter information on your phone. They can also encrypt your files and then ransom them back to you.

Hackers like hacking SIMs because most smartphone users

never realize that hackers hacked their smartphones. Scammers can get away with SIM hacks because, generally, people don't regularly check their phones for viruses, malware, or strange software. Furthermore, they are usually unaware of a problem until they check their crypto wallet balances and realize they are incorrect.

How It's Done

Hackers can access your smartphone by contacting your phone service carrier and impersonating you. They will provide your phone service carrier with your date of birth, social security number, mother's maiden name, etc., so they can get your account information and change it. Another way they get your information is by bribing your phone service carrier's employees to give them the lead. Sadly, they can get your data for less than $200 from most phone service carrier employees.

Spotting a SIM Hack

To avoid having your SIM hacked and having your crypto assets stolen, do the following:

- Never connect your mobile phone to your crypto account.
- Only access your crypto account using a landline or a free Google Voice number.
- Use codes sent to your phone to confirm your crypto account.
- Use a two-factor authentication system on your crypto account.

- If you use your mobile phone, set a unique PIN and security questions on your crypto account.
- Use a strong password on your crypto accounts or get a password manager.
- Use a virtual private network (VPN) to conceal your Internet connection.

VPNs encrypt your IP address. When your IP address is hidden, government agencies, companies, advertisers, and would-be hackers have difficulty locating your electronic device (e.g., laptop, smartphone, desktop) online. Because they cannot quickly identify or track your IP address, they are less likely to be able to steal your personal information, interfere with your crypto transactions, or place cookies and malware on your electronic device. VPNs work on public and private networks. There is a range of prices and plans. For more information on VPNs, please look at ExpressVPN, Mullvad, Nord VPN, SurfShark, hide.me, and Proton VPN.

ASYMMETRICAL GIVEAWAYS

Scammers love to set up asymmetrical giveaways using social media campaigns. In the scams, the scammers promise to give away free crypto tokens to people who send them crypto tokens first. Then, the scammers tell the would-be victims that they will receive significantly more crypto tokens in return after giving up their crypto tokens. Unfortunately, the reality is that after they receive your crypto tokens, you will never hear from them again.

Avoiding Asymmetrical Giveaways

Never send your crypto tokens to someone's crypto wallet with the expectation that they will send them back and reward you by giving you more crypto tokens. Why would anyone ever do that? What do they get from it? There are no free lunches in life. If someone offers you a free lunch, look for the catch.

GENERAL RULES FOR AVOIDING HAVING YOUR CRYPTOCURRENCY STOLEN VIA HACKING OR SCAMS

- Don't tell everyone you have cryptocurrency, especially on social media.
- Avoid direct messages on chats with people you don't know. Usually, the attacker will contact you first.
- Don't download software or click on links that you are not sure are safe and secure.
- Never give anyone your secret seed phrase, private keys, or crypto wallet password.
- Have multiple email accounts for various purposes (e.g., one for accessing exchanges, one for communications, etc.). An attacker might try to access your cryptocurrency accounts on different crypto exchanges by using your email and seeing if they get any results.

PROTECTING YOUR CUSTODIAL CRYPTO ACCOUNTS, PRIVATE KEYS, AND SECRET SEED PHRASES

For custodial wallets and crypto wallets on CEXs, you should use a three-part account authorization system. Unfortunately, the most common two-factor authorization (2FA) system is not secure because it is vulnerable to hacking. Hackers can still hack the three-part system, but it takes more time and is more challenging.

Let's examine the 2FA system, then look at the third part that backs it up.

2FA

In the 2FA system, you cannot access the crypto account without inputting at least two pieces of security data. First, crypto account holders will input their username and password and then be required to input a code sent to their email account or smartphone.

HACKING EMAIL ACCOUNTS

Email accounts have been vulnerable to hacking for some time. We regularly read about data breaches or hackers hacking into email accounts. If you only use 2FA, a hacker can hack into your email, click the "Forgot Password" link (who hasn't forgotten their password at least once?), and reset your password from inside your account. After resetting your password, the hacker will have full access to your crypto account.

SIM SWAPPING

SMS messages are problematic because SIM swapping has become quite common and is very easy. In SIM swapping, a hacker contacts your mobile service carrier and claims to be in distress because of a lost SIM card or smartphone. The hacker will then ask the mobile phone company to switch your phone number to a new SIM card or smartphone. After the carrier changes your phone number to the hacker's SIM or smartphone, the hacker can quickly complete the 2FA authentication process required to access your crypto account.

AUTHENTICATOR APPS

If you use an authenticator app like Google Authenticator, Microsoft Authenticator, or Authy, a hacker will have to go the extra mile to get into your account. These apps are not difficult or time-consuming, but you must set them up on each crypto exchange account. The most important thing to note about authenticator app setup is that you must store your account backup password. You can use the account backup password to regenerate your Authy account if you lose your phone or email access. It would help if you never gave anyone this password, because it is the key to your crypto kingdom.

To prevent problems with the authenticator app backup password and your crypto account secret seed phrase, do the following:

- Copy the backup password as written on the screen to a piece of paper. Make sure that it is easy to read, and use ink that cannot easily fade or paper that cannot degrade quickly over time (e.g., the ink becomes unreadable when wet).
- Copy the backup password twice and place each copy in a different safe location (e.g., a safety deposit box).
- Engrave the password on stainless steel that is acid-proof, fire-proof, and shockproof.
- Store the backup passwords on password-protected USBs.
- Set up an email address that you use only for crypto-related activities. This way, if your hackers gain access to your primary email account, the hacker will not get access to your crypto accounts.
- Never give anyone your secret seed phrase or backup password.
- Never store your secret seed phrase or backup password on a computer, smartphone, tablet, etc.

GUIDELINES FOR STRONG CRYPTO WALLET PASSWORDS

Use passwords that are 12 characters long or longer. As passwords increase in length, they become more robust and secure.

Strong passwords use a mix of uppercase and lowercase letters, special characters, and numbers. The patterns should be random, and the keyboard path to typing it should not be memorable. They should also not include your personal information, location, or anything hackers can guess based on your background or familiarity with you. Also, don't reuse old passwords on the same or different accounts.

GENERATING STRONG PASSWORDS

If you are unsure of how to generate strong passwords, here are some ways you can do it:

- Use a password generator app like NordPass to create your password.
- Use a phrase and abbreviate it.
- Choose random words from the dictionary and combine them using different special characters and numbers.
- Use a famous quote that is abbreviated.
- Use emoticons in your password. Emoticons are combinations of special characters, punctuation, and numbers. Examples:

  :-)   ;-)   :p   :-o   :-I   :-(8-p   :-/   = o

- Use similar passwords for all your accounts but change the beginning or ending so that it is specialized for each type of account.

CHAPTER 7
HOW TO FIND
CRYPTOCURRENCY GEMS

TAKE-HOME Message

Investors primarily use fundamental and technical analysis to decide which cryptocurrencies they want to trade or purchase. Fundamental research focuses on studying the crypto project and estimating its potential for growth, longevity, and market value. In comparison, technical analysis focuses on looking at historical price movements and making predictions about future price movements using the asset's market trends. Ultimately, you should choose an investing/trading strategy that reflects your risk tolerance and perception of assets (e.g., purchasing a piece of the company vs. trading parts of a company).

FUNDAMENTAL ANALYSIS VS. TECHNICAL ANALYSIS

Fundamental Analysis

Fundamental analysis (FA) requires an investor to spend lots of time, energy, and effort studying a company and determine its "true" (AKA intrinsic) market value and growth potential. This analysis is best for people who plan to acquire and hold an asset for more than a year.

It is generally believed to be the best investment strategy for people who want to build generational wealth and become financially independent, according to Warren Buffett, the "Oracle of Omaha," the most famous FA investor.

Technical Analysis

Technical analysis (TA) is most often used by short-term investors/traders because their market success depends on making trades at optimal price points. TA focuses on the historical performance of an asset in the market and uses its prior performance to predict its future price movements. Its tools use trends in price movements, mathematical equations that summarize price movements over time, and other kinds of market signals that traders can identify using computer analysis.

Investors using TA tools to make trading decisions often use more than one to determine the market trend and what trades they should enter and exit. The most famous TA investors are those who made a fortune by successfully trading DOGE (Dogecoin), AMC (Amnext), and COSS (Crypto One-Stop Solution) when they briefly went from low market value to stratospheric levels in 2021.

In this chapter, we will review the basics of FA and TA. Although neither analysis technique can guarantee success in the market as a crypto trader or investor, you should choose the one that fits your interests, lifestyle, and level of time commitment.

CRYPTOCURRENCY FUNDAMENTAL ANALYSIS (FA)

FA looks at a crypto project's operations, management, and future market prospects and helps the investor determine if the crypto token is over- or undervalued. In addition, it measures the aspects of a project that are likely to affect a crypto firm's financial success and longevity.

This analysis technique incorporates a crypto firm's revenue, capital, asset distribution, brand, online community activity, future growth potential, return on equity, liabilities, and other information into the investor's estimation of the value, future potential, and potential longevity of the cryptocurrency issuer.

QUALITATIVE & QUANTITATIVE ANALYSIS

Investors review the key characteristics of the company that issued the cryptocurrency. Some factors considered are its:

- Management
- Token's Competitiveness/Competitive Advantage
- Organizational Structure
- Patents
- Proprietary Technology
- Brand
- Corporate Governance
- Market Niche
- Market Size
- Competitors
- Market Regulation
- Business Cycles
- Financial Statements (e.g., balance sheet, income statement, statement of cash flow)

Operations: Corporate Management, Governance, Organizational Structure

As an investor, you want to know the company's decision-makers and how the company makes decisions. In short, you want to be sure that the decision-makers at the company have the skills and experience necessary to make decisions that will positively impact the value of the cryptocurrency you are purchasing or trading.

- Technological Advantages: Patents, Proprietary Technology, Consensus Algorithm

Crypto firms can issue crypto tokens hosted on different blockchains (e.g., USDT, USDC) or primarily on their blockchains (e.g., BTC, XRP, DOT). You can easily distinguish the success of a cryptocurrency by the market niches they occupy— the greater the utility of a crypto token, the greater its market value and demand. Crypto tokens with limited uses must generate high demand, because if they don't, no one will buy or use them. For a limited token to create high demand, it must occupy an underserved market niche or have users who need its services (e.g., XRP).

The technology incorporated into the operations of a crypto token's ecosystem, issuance, passive investment opportunities, or procedures can also significantly affect its market valuation and reputation.

Crypto investors generally prefer to acquire crypto tokens issued by firms that are not likely to be hacked, become unusable due to faulty operational planning or maintenance, or become obsolete. In summary, all these issues will most likely significantly diminish the demand for cryptocurrency or, if more severe, extinguish its need.

- Tokenomics

Tokenomics refers to the supply, burning, and use of the token. In addition, investors/traders should know if the token has its ecosystem, if it can be used on more than one blockchain, whether it's traded on crypto exchanges, and how the company distributes the token to the public.

- Token Supply

Tokens with a limited supply are likely to increase in value over time, especially if the company burns a notable percentage of tokens annually. Moreover, if a cryptocurrency has an unlimited supply of tokens, you'll want to know:

- How are the tokens being issued?
- How many tokens does the company mint each year?
- How many tokens does the company burn each year?

- Token Accessibility

Tokens bought on CEXs have more credibility than tokens you can only purchase on DEXs because DEXs have lower listing requirements for crypto tokens than CEXs. Due to their relaxed standards, DEXs have more low value and fraudulent tokens than CEXs. So, when investing in crypto tokens, as a beginning investor, protect yourself by focusing on crypto tokens that can be bought on CEXs and have several cryptocurrency pairs. The more cryptocurrency pairs a token has on a CEX, the easier it is to buy/sell/trade.

- Token Distribution

If the token has had an initial coin offering (ICO) or is planning one, then carefully consider the percentage of tokens owned by the founders, development team, and outside investors. If the public does not own the majority of the tokens, then that is a red flag that the token's creators don't have faith in it and that they don't believe that the token will have value over time (i.e., for several years).

When the public does not hold the majority of the tokens or only a few people own them, the token's value can be easily manipulated and quickly dumped for a profit after the token has increased in value. Token issuers who think their token has value and a profitable future have a minority of the tokens distributed to the founders and development team. They spread the bulk of the tokens to the public through different offerings, so current stakeholders cannot buy them up (for the most part) before the general public can purchase the tokens in circulation.

- Brand

Brand refers to the reputation of the token or its blockchain. If a brand is well known and has a good reputation, then its value will likely be higher than is justified by its market characteristics and project potential.

Brand sentimentality can cause people to buy and hold a token with limited use, poor development, and lacking uniqueness (e.g., DOGE, SHIB). Therefore, if you are considering investing in these coins, you should know how much the token's market value depends on people's sentimental feelings.

- Brand Strength: DOGE and Bitcoin

DOGE's market value depends on its community's emotional attachment to the token. Although the token may never rise again to the price levels it hit in the first quarter of 2021, its holders are content to hold it and continue investing in their financial resources. Another example is Bitcoin, which crypto enthusiasts are eager to invest in even if they know little about it.

For both tokens, their brands are so strong that they continue to attract investors despite investors not having carefully studied them or their long-term potential. Like Coca-Cola, Pepsi, Amazon, Nike, Intel, and Apple, these brands drive customer loyalty, and people invest in them simply because of the strength of the brand.

- Community Support and Engagement

When evaluating the value of a token and its future growth potential, its community support and engagement are key factors in determining its actual value and potential. An active, engaged, and growing online community is critical to the mass adoption of a crypto token. Without mass adoption or a growing adoption of a crypto token, the token is not likely to increase in value, liquidity, or accessibility.

A token community's chatter drives interest and demand for the coins. When interest and need in cryptocurrency are high, other potential investors/traders will take interest and invest in the token. In addition, crypto and blockchain project developers are more likely to create a project or app that incorporates crypto-currency into their projects and apps.

- Market Characteristics: Niche, Size, Regulation

When estimating a token's potential growth in value, you must consider the size of the market, the market valuation, the uniqueness of the market, and how regulation affects its operation. For example, if you can easily substitute other tokens for the particular coin of your interest, the coin's niche is too general and heavily regulated, so there probably won't be high demand for it. On the other hand, if the request or need for the token is low, you should not expect its market value to climb very high.

- Financial Statements

Investors/traders using FA will also review the crypto token issuing company's balance sheet, income statement, and cash flow statement.

- Balance Sheet

The balance sheet records a company's assets, liabilities, and equity. The company controls corporate assets, which include cash, inventory, machinery, and buildings. The company's liabilities include short- and long-term loans, corporate bonds, and other types of corporate debt. Equity consists of the corporate shares owned by the company.

- Income Statement

A corporate income statement includes a report on the company's earnings and expenses over a set period and the business's profit. The company can use it to assess the efficiency of the company in generating revenue and profits from its operations and money invested in its operations.

- Statement of Cash Flow

This statement is a record of the company's cash inflow and outflow over some period of time. This statement includes information on the following:

1. Cash from Investing (CFI) – Cash is used to acquire assets and the proceeds from selling other assets (e.g., equipment, buildings, businesses).
2. Cash from Financing (CFF) – Cash proceeds from the issuance and borrowing of funds.
3. Operating Cash Flow (OCF) – Cash proceeds from the day-to-day business operations.

WHITE PAPER REVIEW

Most, if not all, of the information listed in the FA section should be in the crypto token's white paper. If the white paper does not have this information and the development team hasn't issued press releases with the information, you should be wary of investing in the token.

You must decide whether the crypto project looks legitimate or is just one of the thousands of crypto scams separating investors from their money. A poorly written white paper does not indicate that a crypto project will fail. On the other hand, a perfectly written white paper does not guarantee that a crypto project will succeed.

White Papers and Fake Initial Coin Offerings

Be aware that initial coin offerings (ICOs) and other public token offerings are trendy ways of scamming beginning and inexperienced crypto investors out of money. The white papers produced by the scammers and fraudsters look very appealing, generally have terrific graphics, and often are copied from other projects.

The key to figuring out which crypto and blockchain projects are fake and authentic is to look at the project's technical parts, funding, token distribution, online community, completed milestones, and long-term plans.

Fake ICOs tend to:

- Be thinly funded
- Lack an active and engaged online community
- Have huge gaps in information about their technical inner workings
- Distribute the majority of the tokens to people involved in the project
- Not have completed any substantive milestones
- Have a short-term outlook

These are their primary weaknesses because they don't plan on the token increasing in value, being practical, or staying "alive" very long. So instead, they want to sell their token to the public and disappear with their investors' funds.

ON-CHAIN ANALYSIS

When evaluating a blockchain, you should include several factors in your analysis of its revenue-generating potential and performance:

1. Number of Transactions – The transactions processed on the blockchain during specific periods indicate how active the blockchain is and the demand for its services. The total number of transactions will include transferring funds between crypto wallets, so you cannot accept this number at face value.
2. Transactional Value – The value of funds transferred in a transaction or group.
3. Number of Active Addresses – Ways to count the

number of active addresses vary. The easiest way to do this is to count the number of sending and receiving addresses within a set period.

4. Transaction Fees – Look at the transaction fees the blockchain's platform users pay. The higher the costs are bid up at auctions by large platform users, the more successful the platform is.

5. Blockchain Hacks – If the blockchain has been hacked repeatedly, you may want to pass on it. Blockchains with adequate support, good coding, and traffic generally are not easily hacked. Note that cryptocurrency blockchains are not the same as crypto exchanges, so you cannot apply the same reasoning to crypto exchanges. Although you should be wary of a crypto exchange that has been hacked, especially if it has been hacked multiple times.

6. Blockchain Downtime – If the blockchain has had to suspend its activities because it was overwhelmed by transactions or crashed due to platform users' heavy usage of its services, you may want to pass on it. Blockchains may process transactions much slower when traffic is on them, but they should not crash. If the blockchain has been down more than once, you should carefully research the development team and what it has done to stop this from happening in the future.

7. Blockchain Patches – No matter how great the coding of a blockchain is, something will be missed and cause problems. You are not looking for a blockchain with perfect code but one with good coding, vigilant coders and security personnel, and evidence that the operators and developers are finding and fixing problems in the blockchain's code before they cause problems for the platform's users.

FUNDAMENTAL ANALYSIS' 4 BASIC ASSUMPTIONS

FA has four basic assumptions that must be valid or reasonably true for FA to reflect a company's "true" value:

1. The current stock price does not reflect the actual value of the company.
2. The FA value better reflects the company's "true" stock value.
3. Over time, the stock price will reflect the calculated FA value. It is unknown how long it will take for the company's stock price to reflect the FA valuation. It could take days, months, or even years.
4. Investors who focus on specific industries and their companies can calculate the intrinsic value of companies in the industry and find opportunities to buy the stock at discounted prices.

TECHNICAL ANALYSIS (TA)

TA of cryptocurrency is based on the Dow Theory, which has six fundamental principles. The six principles are:

1. The market price of an asset represents the asset's "true" value (including traders' expectations and market sentiment).
2. You would base price movements on the following market trends:
3. Primary/main trends that last from several months to more than a year.
4. You can locate secondary trends in primary/main trends; these last several weeks and are market corrections of the primary/main trends.
5. Minor/short trends that last 1–2 weeks.

6. Primary trends have three consecutive phases, which are:

7. Accumulation – Buyers buy the asset, or sellers sell it. Their market activity doesn't affect the price of the investment.

8. Public Participation – More traders notice and follow the new market trend, and their trading activity causes the asset's price to change rapidly.

9. Distribution – During periods of rampant speculation, experienced traders distribute their holdings.

10. Different TA indices must confirm on another's market signals. The correlation between crypto pairs' movements is something you can observe in the crypto market.

11. There must be an increase in trading volume as the price moves. If the trading volume increases with the price movements, the price follows the market trend. However, if the trading volume decreases as the price movements increase, the price moves against the market trend.

12. A trend continues until there are obvious signals in the market that it will reverse itself. Prices generally follow trends; they don't change them. Reversals in primary trends can be challenging to identify and often resemble secondary movements.

TECHNICAL ANALYSIS (TA) TOOLS

There are five main categories of TA tools. The categories are:

1. Trade Statistics (e.g., Trading Volume)
2. Candlestick Analysis
3. Chart Patterns
4. Resistance and Support Levels
5. Technical Indicators

Traders often use a combination of TA tools to read the market. They do this because if the tools give the trader the same signal, they confirm each other. If two or more tools ensure each other, the trader can be confident that the market predictions about price movements are correct or more likely to be accurate. Furthermore, the tools can indicate the strength of the market trend, and the stronger the market trend, the greater the chances that the trader has correctly read or interpreted it.

TA tools help traders to reduce their market risk and trading errors. However, they do not eliminate all trading risks. For example, traders can never be sure that they have made the correct predictions about the market trend, because they often resemble each other to some extent. Also, traders can never know how long a trend will last and how quickly it will change.

Crypto Is Not Perfectly Suited for TA

Moreover, you cannot entirely predict cryptocurrency market movements based on prior market performance. In addition, you cannot simply correlate crypto assets' price movements to actual world events, economies, or investments; thus, its volatility is even more unpredictable.

GENERAL TA TOOL COMPONENTS

This section will review critical factors used by most TA tools to determine market trends. The elements reviewed are analysis time frame, trading volume, candlesticks, support and resistance levels, and chart patterns (e.g., bullish, bearish, reversal, breakout).

Analysis Time Frame

. . .

There is no ideal period for observing the price movements of a crypto token, which means that the observation period primarily depends on your trading strategy.

Traders will focus on different lengths of time because they are engaged in short-term or long-term trading. So, let's look at how the time for market observation changes based on the type of trader.

- Scalpers enter and exit traders quickly (within 1–5 minutes).
- Intraday traders enter and exit trades within a day. They usually review 5-minute, 15-minute, and 60-minute market charts.
- Position traders prefer long-term trading, which runs from 1 day to several weeks.

Trade within concise time frames is often better for volatile, highly speculative markets.

Trading Volume

Trading volume refers to the number of crypto tokens transacted within a specific period and is used to indicate the strength of a market trend. More robust trends have higher trading volumes, and weak trends have low trading volumes.

CANDLESTICKS

Candlestick charts are very popular with experienced and inexperienced investors. The candlesticks show the price movements of an asset during a set period.

Candles have a body, are red or green, and have a maximum of two shadows.

- Green candlesticks

The bottom is the opening price, and the top is the closing price. The closing price is higher than the opening price, so it is considered bullish.

- Red candlesticks

The bottom is the closing price, and the top is the opening price. Because the opening price is higher than the closing price, it is considered bearish.

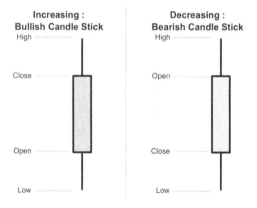

Image originally from Probe-meteo.com, CC BY-SA 3.06.[5]

Image "How to Read Candlesticks" from Financial Freedom Trading.[6]

Image by Mohamed Mahmoud Hassan on PublicDomainPictures.[7]

CANDLESTICK STRENGTH

The asset's price changes result from aggressive buying and selling in the market and the volume of orders. If there are many sell orders at the current price, the price will decrease. However, if there are many buy orders at the current price, the price will rise.

In short, when sell orders exceed buy orders, the asset's price drops. But conversely, the worth rises when buyer orders exceed the seller orders.

Because a great deal of market buying and selling occurs based on emotion, the candlesticks, which illustrate the aggressiveness of buying and selling of an asset, show the price moves of an investment and the emotional state of the people trading the asset.

You can see a candlestick's strength in its structure; they have a body and zero to a maximum of two shadows. The shadows are lines extending from a candlestick's top and bottom.

Let's review the different candlestick strengths.

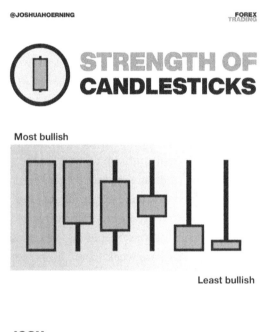

Image "Strength of Candlesticks" from Financial Freedom Trading.[8]

1. The strongest candlestick has a long body with no upper or lower shadow. This type of candle signals that the current price move will continue. The price move could still change direction, but it is doubtful. (Very Strong Signal)
2. Still a strong candlestick, this one has a long body and short upper/lower shadow in the opposite direction of the price move. The price will likely continue to move

in the same direction but has a slight chance of changing. (Strong Signal)

3. Candlestick with a mid-sized body with mid-sized upper and lower shadows. This is a moderate signal. The current price move is likely to continue. However, there is a significant risk that the direction of the price will change. (Moderately Strong Signal)

4. With a smaller-than-mid-sized body but not a short one and two mid-length upper and lower shadows, this moderate signal is the least promising in the average strength range. There is a significant chance that the direction of the price will change, but it is more likely that it will continue to move in the same direction. (Weak Moderate Signal)

5. This candlestick has a small body and one long upper/lower shadow extending in the direction of the price move. The candlestick's opening and closing price and close signal are weak. There is an excellent chance that the price move will change direction.

6. The weakest candlestick signal. It has a thin body with a long upper/lower shadow that extends in the direction of the price move. This candlestick signals that the investor should prepare for a change in price direction. (Weakest Signal)

CHART PATTERNS

Candlesticks create chart patterns traders can use to gauge, read, and predict the market. As you improve your ability to read and interpret chart patterns, you will place strategic trades and reduce your trading risks. Most importantly, you'll have a better chance of making more profitable trades. The trade patterns that traders look for are:

- Bullish Candlestick Pattern

This trading signal means that the asset's price is rising. If the trader can enter the market at a good position, at low cost, and sell at major price peaks, you will profit from the trade when you maximize the price peaks or just after it peaks.

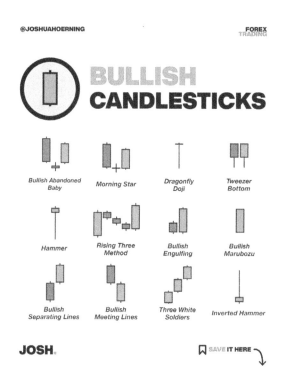

Image "Bullish Candlesticks" from Financial Freedom Trading.[9]

BEARISH CANDLESTICK PATTERN

This pattern signals that the asset's price is falling and that it is not the time to buy it. If possible, sell the investment before the price decreases to where you lose money, make no profit, or make very little profit. Conversely, when the asset's price hits its lowest low, that is the perfect time to buy the asset and then sell it when the price peaks again.

Image "Bearish Candlesticks" from Financial Freedom Trading.[10]

BULLISH REVERSAL PATTERN

A bullish reversal pattern signals that the asset's falling price will change direction and rise. It's a reversal pattern because the bearish trend changes into a bullish trend.

BEARISH REVERSAL PATTERN

A bearish reversal pattern signals the asset's rising price will change direction and fall. It's a reversal pattern because the bullish trend changes into a bearish trend.

The Head and Shoulders chart pattern shows you bullish and bearish reversal patterns. Also, there is an image of a Head and Shoulder chart pattern found in Bitcoin market data.

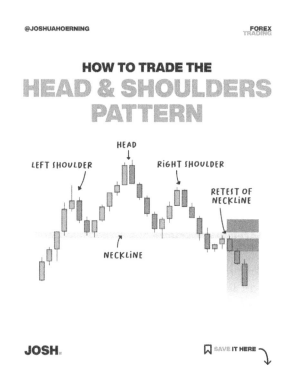

Image "How to Trade the Head & Shoulders Pattern" from Financial Freedom Trading. [11]

Image from Crypto News, June 10, 2019.[12]

CONTINUATION TREND PATTERN

This signal means that the market trend will continue for an unknown period of time (i.e., more than one bar). It allows traders to enter/exit their positions and set up lucrative trades.

In the Head and Shoulders chart pattern above, the price breaks through the support line and continues downward (bearish trend).

SUPPORT AND RESISTANCE LEVELS

Market charts with candlesticks have support and resistance lines. A support line is a line you can draw along the bottom of the candlesticks. It represents the general direction of the low prices over some time. The resistance line is the line you can draw along the tops of the candles.

Support symbolizes the strength of an asset pushing up against market pressure for its price to drop. The stronger the support, the less likely the price will fall below it.

The resistance symbolizes the strength of the asset to keep its price from rising. The stronger the opposition, the less likely the asset price will rise above it.

The support and resistance lines form common shapes on the

market charts. Initially, it may be difficult for you to "see" shapes in the charts, but with time and practice, you will be able to identify different chart shapes and what they tell you about the market trend of the asset.

You can observe significant and minor support and resistance in the image below.

Image "Major & Minor Support and Resistance" from Financial Freedom Trading.[13]

BREAKOUT PATTERN

When an asset's price falls below the support line or rises above the resistance line, the price breaks out of the trend. If you can predict a price breakout, you can make some very profitable trades. The chart below shows some common breakout patterns.

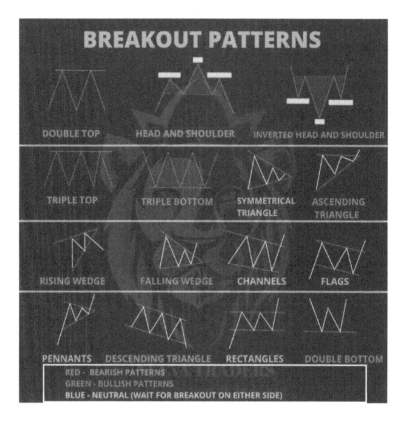

Image "Breakout Patterns" from Financial Freedom Trading.[14]

OTHER TA TOOLS

There are other TA analysis tool indicators that you can use to read and interpret the crypto market. Although we cannot review them here, you can research this list of the most popular ones. You should use the ones you feel most comfortable with, trust, and feel confident using to guide your crypto trading decisions.

The most commonly used TA indicators are:

- On-Balance Volume (OBV)
- Accumulation/Distribution Line (A/D Line)
- Average Directional Index (ADX)
- Aroon Indicator
- Moving Average Convergence Divergence (MACD)
- Relative Strength Index (RSI)
- Stochastic Indicator

PAPER TRADING

Are you ready to start trading crypto?

Would you feel more comfortable if you had a demo account from which you could practice trading crypto tokens using fake money?

Well, you can practice your trading skills using paper trading. Paper trading is a demo account with fake money you use to make trades. After making the trades, you can observe the results of your market decisions and develop strategies to optimize your market performance.

Many companies have free demo accounts, so you should not pay for one. If possible, get a demo account with a company that you are interested in working with in the future. Remember, many firms allow trading more than cryptocurrency on their platforms.

Some companies that you may want to consider if you decide to open a paper trading are:

- Webull
- eToro
- AvaTrade
- Interactive Brokers
- TradeStation
- Thinkorswim

- Capital.com
- Tradier
- FOREX.com

FINDING YOUR NEEDLE IN THE HAYSTACK

You are now ready to begin developing your crypto token trading skills. There are thousands of crypto tokens on the market, so you have many options. If you prefer to work with crypto tokens with a track record and lots of market data, consider the ones with the highest market caps.

Using your paper trading account or whatever way you choose to practice trading and testing your trading strategies, focus on one or more of the following crypto tokens:

- Bitcoin Native Token (BTC)
- Bitcoin Cash Native Token (BCH)
- Ethereum Native Token (Ether)
- Polkadot Native Token (DOT)
- Decentraland Native Token (MANA)
- Dogecoin Native Token (DOGE)
- Cardano Native Token (ADA)
- Tether Native Token (USDT)

BUILD YOUR CRYPTO WEALTH NOW!

You have everything you need to develop and improve your crypto trading skills. Get started today! When comfortable and confident with paper trading, begin investing in crypto tokens.

Note, don't be a forever paper trader!

· · ·

At some point, you will have to commit to crypto trading and invest your own money.

If you struggle to begin actively trading, set a date for trading and invest a small amount of money in your trade. Eventually, you must "rip the Band-Aid off" and expose yourself to the crypto market, for better or worse.

Remember: With experience and (some) luck comes great opportunity and wealth.

CHAPTER 8
STRATEGICALLY PROFIT FROM CRYPTOS AND THE KEYS TO CREATING YOUR MULTI-GENERATIONAL WEALTH

TAKE-HOME Message

Crypto investors who want to become millionaires and create multi-generational wealth must be disciplined, dispassionate, and record-keeping investors to set goals, milestones, and market entry/exit strategies. Overall, the best plan for accumulating wealth as a crypto investor is to invest in crypto assets that are promising long-term.

WHAT IS MULTI-GENERATIONAL WEALTH?

When you have achieved multi-generational wealth, it means that you have built up a sizable fortune in savings and investments that is also resilient, self-perpetuating, and, more importantly, secure. As a result, your children, grandchildren, and great-grandchildren will benefit from the wealth you have created in your lifetime. It's the legacy you want to leave behind, knowing that your grandchildren will benefit from your investments and hard work many years later.

Nowadays, the average person can create multi-generational wealth using the multiplier effect of crypto investing. The opportunities are still abundantly available; in 2021, more than 68 cryptocurrencies increased their values by more than 1,000%.[15] This rare opportunity has not been available to the average person for generations. However, creating multi-generational wealth is not a get-rich-quick scheme. You must be in it for the long run; achieving it requires staying the course and not letting your emotions trip you up.

For the first time in history, cryptocurrency has democratized the opportunity to become a millionaire. Moreover, regarding wealth preservation, cryptocurrencies can be foundational to keeping families' fortunes intact and passing them on to future generations. With a market cap of greater than $400 billion, there are an estimated 18,000 new millionaires due to Bitcoin's unparallel rise.[16] Furthermore, the rise of bitcoin may only be in its infancy and is happening at a global scale, which means there is a rare opportunity to accumulate a massive amount of wealth; historically, wealth transfers have happened mainly at regional scales.

Due to cryptocurrencies' unguessable and hack-proof 256-SHA encryption key—a secure hash algorithm (SHA) that transforms a string of data into precisely 256 bits of data—cryptocurrencies are an incredible tool for securing generational wealth because they are virtually impossible to confiscate. You can memorize the secret seed phrase to generate your crypto wallet, and the seed phrase can be handed down to future generations, perhaps even without a third-party trust. Furthermore, the finite number of coins minted in specific cryptocurrencies is a significant hedge against inflation. Can you imagine leaving 1 Bitcoin for your grandkids and having that value accumulate over time to be worth $1 million or $5 million when they become adults? By storing your accumulated wealth in cryptocurrencies, you have a better chance of safeguarding and growing your family fortune and guarding against the rise of inflation for years to come.

Keep your wealth tree growing by making sure that it has

deep roots. Deep roots come from making sound investments in growth sectors with good return on investment. Cryptocurrency, blockchain technology, and crypto-related industries are not going away. They are evolving to fill unmet needs in different markets and to more efficiently manage commercial transactions.

Now, you are probably wondering how viable cryptocurrency is as a long-term investment because its market rises and falls suddenly with no apparent reason as to the cause of the market shifts. Well, this happens in the stock market too. However, there are some potential explanations for the stock market's shifts because the stock market is tied to real-world, tangible assets and services. It has been hard for most investors to beat the stock market, despite the information available about companies listed on stock exchanges and the 24/7 news broadcasts about every international event that may affect it.

Wise investors know that when the market is in turmoil and they are uncertain about what to do with their crypto investments, they should do nothing. Your due diligence in selecting your crypto investments, your studies of market activity, your (ideally) detachment from it, and your predetermined investment exit plans will tell you what to do. But most of the time, you should do nothing. Just bide your time and watch the market reset itself.

Investors with long-term mindsets don't care about the daily vagaries of the market. Instead, they look at the big picture, their investment performance over time, and opportunities to add valuable investments to their portfolio. For example, Warren Buffett is a very successful investor who invests for the long-term (decades). He does not sell off his assets when they suddenly drop in value or when there is a bear market. Instead, when the market is in the basement, he goes shopping for great investments that produce sound, sustainable returns over time. In short, there has to be congruence between your intentions and actions. Making choices out of fear is incongruent with a long-term investment strategy.

At this point, you have decided to adopt a long game and create multi-generational wealth (otherwise, why are you reading this book?). However, your resolve to be detached and confident, practice due diligence, and watch the markets has spurred you to press on and master the techniques and mindset of crypto millionaires.

ADOPT A LONG-TERM INVESTMENT GAME PLAN

Your Decision-Making Process

Before you can put your long-term investment strategy to work, you have to have good information. However, suppose you base your decisions on erroneous or poorly reported news. In that case, your potential actions are faulty, and the outcome—whichever plan you choose—will likely not produce the desired results.

Remember: Choosing between the lesser of two evils is still choosing something evil. Good information sources will inform you of your best options to achieve your goals. Choosing between good/promising options will likely help you stay the course and create multi-generational wealth within your lifetime.

There are millions of ways to make a million dollars. But unfortunately, people rarely do it because they do not take action.

Decide Your Risk Tolerance and Preferred Investment Type

Take the time to research and find the best crypto investments for you. Finding an investment that works for you means that if you have a low tolerance for risk and limited funds to invest in the crypto market, you don't want to invest in derivatives, contracts for differences (CFDs), or high-risk crypto tokens (e.g., initial coin offerings [ICOs]). However, if you have money to burn and can tolerate high-risk investments without becoming depressed, then high-risk, highly speculative crypto investments might be a good option. Likewise, if you are entering the market and want to invest in more conservative assets with lower risk and market history, put your money into legacy tokens (e.g., Bitcoin, Ether).

Investment Goals

The goal of your investment comes first, then figuring out what to invest in and when to sell becomes easy. Each time you make an investment, write down the goal of that investment. For instance, if your goal is to invest $1,000 and pay off $4,500 in debt, then make that your focus. However, if your goal is to generate multi-generational wealth, you must find suitable projects, strategically invest your capital, and look for promising long-term investments. Also, track the progress of each asset so that you can identify the ones that are the most profitable and those that you may want to exit or avoid in the future.

TRADING VS. HODLING

Most people favor one of three different crypto investing strategies. The three strategies are day trading, HODLing, and a mixture.

Trading

• • •

Trading often refers to day trading or short-term crypto investing. Traders try to enter and exit positions at specific times to earn profits quickly. Before taking a particular position, the trader determines the timing of trades, the market prices of the buy/sell, and the tolerance of high levels of market volatility while seeking short-term gain.

Although trading can be highly lucrative for some, most people lose money or have their gains wiped out by their losses. Plus, trading success depends on making the right decision at the right place at the right time. It also requires traders to remain dispassionate, act independently, and stay above the market fray as they execute their trading strategies. In short, successful crypto traders usually don't travel in packs or follow the herd.

HODLing

HODLing, or Hold On for Dear Life-ing, is when crypto investors invest in crypto tokens for the long term. The long term may be 1 year, 10 years, or more. Regardless of the investment period, they commit to holding the crypto tokens and wait for the tokens to mature or the predetermined time to sell them. HODLers pride themselves on watching the market, making sound investment decisions, and not being affected by the market-driven decisions of most day traders.

HODLing cryptocurrency is one of the great pillars of building and retaining generational wealth, along with the other pillars, including real estate, precious metals, stocks, bonds, and life insurance.

Instead, the HODLers band together, support one another, and ride out the market volatility as they wait for their tokens to increase in value or return to their high market valuation. The most legendary HODLers are the Warren Buffetts of the crypto world. They have been holding their Bitcoin and Ether tokens since they bought them after the ICO. Keeping their tokens for years has made some of them billionaires, more millionaires, and a large number a tidy profit. Still, to reach that level, they had to hold the tokens and believe their value would continue to rise over time. Unfortunately, most people who initially invested in Bitcoin and Ethereum did not hold this belief and instead cashed out as soon as they had the opportunity to get a decent profit from selling them.

HODL YOUR WAY TO GENERATIONAL WEALTH

If you want to HODL your way to accumulating generational wealth, you must first find a crypto token worth investing in for years. Because thousands of crypto tokens are on the market, hundreds of new coins launch yearly, and the majority become dead coins less than two years after being launched, this is no easy feat. Although there is a fair bit of luck involved in finding the tokens that will mature in value over time and turn you into a millionaire, there are some standard things that you should do to increase your chances of identifying them.

Doing the following will increase your chances of finding HODL-worthy crypto tokens.

• Read the White Paper

The white paper of a crypto token project should tell you in detail why blockchain developers created the project, its purpose, how it will develop over time, the people who will be interested in it, and how the development team plans to maintain and expand the project. Although promoters of the blockchain use white papers to be a part of the marketing effort, they are also supposed to be detailed writings about the usefulness of the token and its blockchain. If the white paper lacks detailed information about the token, it is a poorly written document and may be a sign that the project is poorly put together and not likely to last the test of time. Lastly, if it is too similar to another token's white paper, that should raise some alarms. New blockchain developers should not copy white papers or imitate one another. Lack of authenticity in the white paper is a major red flag.

- Research the Founders and Development Team

To drive a token's development, launch, release, and maintenance, you need founders and a development team with a vision, a background in cryptocurrency and blockchain technology, and some connections to the industry. They should also have an active online presence that you can trace. For example, they should have profiles on LinkedIn, be part of online crypto forums, and have been part of at least one crypto project. The founders and development team don't have to have a flawless technology background; as a group, they should complement one another and provide the skills, talents, knowledge, and expertise necessary to develop, launch, and maintain a crypto token.

- Assess the Project's Milestones

Blockchain developers create crypto projects for long-term investment, usefulness, and value and should have milestones laid out before they launch a blockchain. Blockchain developers should have achieved some initial landmarks; moreover, there should be evidence that the team is actively progressing towards achieving the next milestone and setting the stage for attaining additional milestones. In short, the developers should set aside capital to fund the maintenance and development of the token, a system to generate more revenue to invest in the token, and an active effort to reinvest funds into the token and the services it provides its users. Absent this kind of financial investment in the token, it will most likely not be an excellent long-term investment.

- Investigate the Token's Community

Crypto tokens that will last need a community that will support them, spread information about them, create demand for them, and have an interest in holding them. You can find crypto communities on Twitter, Reddit, Discord, and Facebook. If you want to invest in a token, pay attention to the chatter and discussion about the token. However, you should not assume that everything you hear or read about the token of interest is authentic. There may be some golden nuggets of information mixed in with the forum discussions that will give you some leads on where to research the token, the project's intended longevity, and whether or not anyone thinks the token is a scam.

Note that if you have noticed that the community focuses on hyping the token and driving demand for it, you should be wary of it. Scammers hyping tokens is commonly done in pump-and-dump schemes and other scams that seek to drive up a token's value so that a small group of investors who hold a large number of tokens can sell them for a price higher than justified by the market. These scams only reward those who cash out before the bottom drops out of the market. People who buy the token after it significantly increases in value or who don't sell before its market price drops tend to lose money or make very little profit from investing.

- Follow the Money

Before investing in a token, research who holds the majority of the tokens. If the founders and development team plan for the project to increase in value, be a long-term investment, and have a large community, then they need the public to own the bulk (greater than 50%) of the tokens.

Stay away from tokens and projects where the founders, development team, and big investors own most of the tokens. If the public owns only 30% of the tokens, then the project stake-holders will likely dump the tokens when their value rises to a certain level. In addition, if the founders and development team require investors to exchange high-value tokens for their newly launched token, it may be a scam. After enough investors have exchanged their Bitcoin, Ether, XRP, etc., for the new token, the project operators can shut the project down and disappear with the high-value tokens. Unfortunately, in such cases, the investors are left holding worthless tokens and have no way to get any justice.

- The Usefulness of the Token

Tokens with a long-term market future must be helpful. The tokens should serve some unmet needs in the crypto market. If the token dominates the niche it was designed to fill, there will be a need and demand for it. Furthermore, what is unique about the token and its blockchain will enable it to develop a strong market position and maintain it.

For example, Ether was created to be used in transactions, held for value, and as a reward. Moreover, as the Ethereum blockchain has evolved to host NFTs, smart contracts, and DeFi transactions, the value and demand for Ether have continued to rise. Plus, Ether's development team and founders continue to push for Ether to be competitive against later developed blockchains and crypto tokens.

Finally, later, blockchain developers developed tokens and

blockchains that were Ethereum-compatible so that their users could benefit from the new innovative blockchain and not lose the benefits of having access to the Ethereum blockchain. Thus, it is clear that holding Ether as a long-term investment makes sense.

HOW TO HODL

If you plan on HODLing your way to being a millionaire or creating multi-generational wealth, you must approach it with the proper mindset. In this section, I list things you must do to have a wealth-building mindset as a crypto investor.

THINK LONG-TERM

Remember, this is a long-term investment strategy and not a get-rich-quick scheme. The real secret here is time in the market. Your investment in technology will service masses of people and create compounded value yearly. So, what you give now might pay you back 10-fold, 100-fold, or even 1,000-fold in the future.

YOU MUST PLANT THE SEEDS OF WEALTH

Your initial investment in cryptocurrency is like planting a seed, letting it take root, and reaping the rewards of its growth over time.

HODL-WORTHY CRYPTOCURRENCIES

Below are several cryptocurrencies that are HODL-worthy, meet the criteria that score very high on our fundamental analysis, and are poised for the massive multiplier effect for long-term investing. Please follow the link at the beginning of the book for our free gift. The report provides an in-depth analysis of these phenomenal cryptocurrencies and the unique qualities of their revolutionary blockchains.

- Bitcoin Cash (BCH)
- Cardano (ADA)
- Theta (THETA) & Theta Fuel (TFUEL)

The information in this book references an opinion and is for informational purposes only. Market understanding, appropriate asset allocation, experience, and knowledge are prerequisites for proper investing.

In any market, especially the digital asset market, it is essential to understand the risks and dynamics of your investments. It is also important to understand these risks on a level at which you can protect your assets. If you are unaware of this information or unsure of how to protect your investment, please seek professional investment advice.

To ensure your long-term success and survival in the financial markets, please do not overexpose yourself, and remember to be aware of your risk tolerance.

DOLLAR-COST AVERAGE YOUR WAY INTO HODLING

Since HODLing is playing the long game and not about getting rich overnight, your strategy is to dollar-cost into the blockchain you have chosen to invest.

What is dollar-cost averaging? *Forbes* magazine defines it as "a strategy to manage price risk when buying stocks, exchange-traded funds (ETFs), or mutual funds. Instead of investing in a particular security at one time, with a single purchase price, with dollar-cost averaging you divide up the amount of money you'd like to invest and buy small quantities over time at regular intervals. This decreases the risk that might pay too much before market prices drop."[17]

The strategy is to buy into your HODL-worthy crypto at

intervals in small quantities and not to time your way into the market. When the market has dipped, buy in a little more; when there are significant dips, buy even more. But always remember that this is money you can afford to lose or money you don't need for any reason immediately.

BE PREPARED TO RIDE OUT THE HIGHS AND LOWS

The crypto market is highly volatile. If you want to reap the rewards of HODLing, you must stay on the course during the market volatility and do nothing while you watch your token's market value steeply rise or fall. But being steadfast in the investment strategy is based on sound research, as discussed earlier. Because the crypto market is not connected to the fundamental world market's volatility, it is difficult to time and predict. In short, have an investment strategy for each token you purchase and stick to it unless market conditions or other factors merit changing your plans for it. Remember, you base your success on your decisions about when to buy in and sell. Therefore, your success is ultimately your responsibility.

CASH ON HAND

Keep 20% of your investment capital in fiat currency (e.g., USD, EUR, GBP) for buying tokens during dips in the market or when other great opportunities come along.

SELL TARGETS FOR PROFIT-TAKING

Set your sell targets and stick to them. Remember, you base your sell targets on the financial goals you are trying to achieve (e.g., paying off debts, tuition). Don't make the targets too outrageous (e.g., a billion dollars, buying an NBA team).

Note that this is one of the keys to profitable investing.

Successful investing depends on setting the right sell target, not selling at the right time.[18] So, keep an eye on your sell targets when cryptocurrency prices rise. When the market prices rise to your sell target, SELL a certain percentage of your holdings from 10 to 20%. Please note that some cryptocurrency exchanges offer automatic sell options to sell at a specified price. However, *don't sell your entire position*, because the coin prices may increase again. For example, let's say you invested $1,000 in a token, and when the market goes up, your investment is now $2,000 instead of selling your entire position, which is $2,000. You sell 20% of your position, which is $400, and you still have $1,600 invested. When your coin price doubles again and goes up to $3,200, sell another 20% for a $640 profit. So, your earnings are $400 and $640, which is greater than your initial $1,000 investment—and you still have $2,560 invested. As the price of your coin continues to uptick, continue to sell 10% to 20% of your holding incrementally. Once the market starts to downtick, you can decide whether or not to put the gains back in with dollar-cost averaging or use the profits to pay off or buy whatever you had set for your financial goals. Remember, this is a long game; it can take months or even years to reach your sell target. Be patient, knowing you planted the seeds of wealth and are reaping the rewards.

You must also remember that you base your sell targets on a coin's value. If you have a low-value token, it is ridiculous to expect its market price to rise to Bitcoin's level. Of course, that could happen, but you should set realistic sell targets for your tokens based on their potential market success and demand.

Join a Community

Don't go it alone! Millions of crypto investors worldwide are just starting, learning the market, and trying to build multi-generational wealth. You can learn from them, be supported, and be encouraged, but you must make an effort to be a part of the crypto community. You may find some tremendous investing groups, investing gurus, or discussion forums online and in your area. Open yourself to meeting crypto enthusiasts and expanding your crypto network.

Let's revisit your HODL game plan:

- The best way to get into your HODL game plan is to dollar-cost average into your crypto investment. Don't go in all at once.
- Set your sell targets as early as possible before significant market upticks. Always keep track of the original purchase price of your cryptos.
- Remember, cash is a position. Always keep a cash reserve for periods to buy into a dip.

REINVEST YOUR PROFITS

Reinvesting is a great challenge for an investor because it means that the investor has successfully profited from the market. However, it also means you must decide when you've made enough profit and when you'll want to wait for more profit.

Before withdrawing profits from your investment, ask yourself the following questions:

- Why did I buy this token?
- What was my investment goal with this crypto token?
- Am I comfortable holding onto this token, or would it be better for me to sell a part of my investment?
- At what point am I comfortable taking profits (50%, 100%, 300%, 500%, etc.)?
- Is there a better investment opportunity for my earnings?

After you have decided to remove a portion of your profits from your investment, you should immediately reinvest it. However, before reinvesting it, you should have thoroughly researched your options and made the best decision given your goals, finances, and time constraints.

Some investments that you may want to consider when reinvesting your profits are:

- Crypto mining
- Investing in new crypto tokens
- Rental property
- Paying off your current debts (e.g., credit card, mortgage, school loans)
- HODLing

If you prefer not to sell your crypto tokens and want to profit from your crypto tokens while still holding them, you can do the following:

- Loan your crypto tokens to other crypto investors (i.e., P2P loans)
- Engage in short-term crypto trades for quick profits, where you buy the tokens for a low price on one exchange and immediately sell them for a higher price on another exchange (i.e., arbitrage)

DIVERSIFY YOUR PORTFOLIO

When you reinvest your profits, your goal should be to maximize your gains, minimize your losses, and reduce your overall risk. To hedge against downturns in the market, try to invest in assets that are affected by different market conditions. Also, you would benefit by diversifying your investments in asset classes other than the stock and crypto markets.

WHAT NOT TO DO WHEN INVESTING IN CRYPTOS

Most crypto investors fail because they do not maintain a calm, neutral disposition when managing their crypto investments. Despite their intentions to stick to their investment strategy, they tend to become victims of FUD (fear, uncertainty, doubt) and FOMO (fear of missing out). Let's examine FUD and FOMO to know if you are falling prey to them.

FUD

Most crypto investors are emotional traders. Their emotions tend to dictate how they respond to changes in the market. Interestingly, FUD can affect individuals, investing groups, and communities—and can even be a feeling that characterizes the market.

- **Fear** – Fear stems from being preoccupied with the idea that you will financially suffer or not be able to maximize your financial position like other crypto traders if you do not do what they are doing in the market. It is also a feeling caused by a lack of confidence in your investing strategy, intuition, or process.
- **Uncertainty** – Uncertainty is a feeling that is hard to contain and compartmentalize in crypto investing because crypto markets are volatile, unpredictable, not connected to real-world demands, and highly speculative. No one can be certain about anything in the crypto world. Moreover, crypto token values can increase by 1,000% in less than a month and fall by more than 5,000% weeks later. Not knowing whether a token price will rally again, when it will rally again,

and how long it will stay strong drives the crippling uncertainty that thwarts some of the best investment plans and strategies implemented by the most conscientious and committed investors.

- **Doubt** – Doubt is the insidious feeling that afflicts some despite their best efforts to invest in a rational, calculated way. Investors may obsess over whether they have done enough to safeguard their investments, minimize losses, and maximize gains. Furthermore, this feeling is hard to root out or contain when the volatility and unpredictability of the crypto market renders your well-thought-out investment plans and strategies pointless. Unfortunately, potentially great investors succumb to second-guessing themselves because they want to avoid the market losses suffered in the past and make that last-minute investment decision that saves them from being financially decimated like some of their crypto investing peers.

Defeating FUD

You can conquer FUD by doing the following:

- Set clear and achievable investment goals and milestones.
- Maintain a diversified portfolio.
- Recognize when FUD is overtaking you and develop coping mechanisms for it. Your goal is to reduce it significantly—if not eliminate it—and contain it.
- Set up guidelines for when you will take specific

actions in the market and try not to deviate from your plans except in rare instances.

- Keep a journal of when you've traded assets, why you traded them, and the outcome of your trades.
- Stay up-to-date on the market and the crypto assets you have in your investment portfolio. Your knowledge of crypto markets and your market trading experience will help you keep FUD away and prevent you from falling victim to it.

FOMO

FOMO, or "fear of missing out," drives much of crypto investing. Most investors dream of turning a few hundred thousand dollars into millions by purchasing the correct crypto token (e.g., Bitcoin, Ether, Dogecoin, Shiba). It is a powerful driving force that creates some crypto casualties and potentially lots of economic mayhem as more lay people become crypto investors.

- FOMO Creates the Perfect Prey for Crypto Scammers and Fraudsters

Crypto scammers and fraudsters profit handsomely from FOMO as they push their Ponzi schemes, pyramid schemes, rug pulls, pump-and dump schemes, shilling schemes, and other fraudulent schemes. Unfortunately, people desire not to be excluded from the investment party. Unfortunately, this desire will have many throwing caution to the wind and making bad decisions using limited knowledge without much time to truly consider their investment decision from multiple perspectives.

- FOMO: The False Cure for Economic Uncertainty

FOMO is essentially a herd mentality that deprives investors of the proper mindset to make sound investment decisions. FOMO is pushing lay investors into crypto investing without understanding cryptocurrency and blockchain technology. During these times of economic instability and global economic downturns, people are looking for alternative sources of income to support themselves, fund their retirements, and leave something behind for their descendants.

- FOMO Pushes Lay Investors to Invest Irresponsibly

As everyday people read about crypto investors who have paid off their mortgages, school loans, credit card debt, and school tuition, they too want a chance to earn that kind of money. Unfortunately, most lay investors who are entering the crypto market do not understand the risks, don't carefully research their investments, and don't have clear investing strategies and goals. In short, they are the perfect victims for sophisticated scammers and fraudsters looking for easy prey. Furthermore, many are going into debt to invest in cryptocurrency (e.g., bank loans, credit card cash withdrawals). Unfortunately, credit investment is a contraindicated strategy, because crypto investors can lose all their investment capital at any time. Now, sadly, we are seeing investors risking their retirement funds and ability to pay their living expenses (e.g., mortgages, utility bills) for the opportunity to possibly earn a profit from investing in cryptocurrency.

- FOMO Lowers Investors' Inhibitions

FOMO lowers investors' inhibitions to making risky investment decisions. But unfortunately, in response to FOMO, they are more likely to make impulsive decisions, take more significant risks than they can afford, and engage in poorly reasoned conduct. So, while crypto enthusiasts are thrilled that more and more people are buying cryptocurrency, there is tremendous concern that new investors are risking too much of their savings. New and inexperienced investors cannot walk away from their crypto losses without extreme regret and are irresponsibly participating in the crypto market.

Defeating FOMO

To defeat FOMO, you must accept that you can't ride every crypto wave. You must also acknowledge that crypto investing is gambling and that there are risks in the market, just like all the other investors, and that sometimes the best investment plans and strategies don't always work. Still, you cannot just wildly follow everyone else because it appears they are doing well and have mastered the market. Accept that you must make well-reasoned, carefully researched decisions, considering your investment goals and milestones to defeat FOMO. For a crypto investor to become a millionaire and create multi-generational wealth, YOLO ("you only live once"") and *carpe diem* ("seize the day") are also not investing slogans that you should embrace.

DECIDE TO TAKE ACTION!

The quality of information and the reputation of the source of information comes from your perception. When advice is free, people often dismiss it and fail to act on it. However, when they must sacrifice time, money, and energy to get it, it becomes more valuable, and people are more likely to act on it and assign it a great value. Thus, when you have committed yourself to something, you are more likely to follow through with action.

At this time, you have committed time, money, and thought to learn about crypto investing and how to create multi-generational wealth. However, to complete your journey to achieve your goal, you must do one thing:

Take action now!!!

CHAPTER 9
YOUR GUIDE ON
CRYPTOCURRENCY TAXES

TAKE-HOME Message

The IRS expects crypto investors to pay taxes on their crypto investments. Although the tax reporting requirements, taxation, and tax triggers are still being developed, you are, by law, required to report on your crypto assets, holdings, and liquidation.

Information presented in this chapter is not tax advice but tax education.

This beginner's guide to crypto investing can only give you the basics to begin your crypto investing journey. In this chapter, you will review the basics of crypto taxation and what you must do to be tax compliant in the US. As with anything essential, you should seek tax guidance from a tax lawyer, tax accountant, or tax preparer who has experience working with cryptocurrency.

THE INTERNAL REVENUE SERVICE AND CRYPTO TAXATION

The Internal Revenue Service (IRS) (AKA Uncle Sam) wants its share of your crypto profits. Fortunately, you can deduct your crypto losses from your capital gains and income taxes. The highest capital gains tax you will pay is 20%, and the maximum income tax you'll pay is 37%. Although some tax guidelines regarding crypto transactions are clear, others are vague. For example, it is unclear whether the IRS will tax certain crypto transactions (e.g., DeFi protocols) shortly.

WITH CRYPTOCURRENCY COMES TAX LIABILITY

Cryptocurrency provides you with a tremendous opportunity to accumulate immense amounts of wealth. But unfortunately, it can also have you end up in tax audits and pay enormous fees and penalties for not paying your crypto taxes.

As with all investments, the IRS wants its cut of your wealth and to know about your crypto assets. To properly report this information, you must keep records of everything you do with your crypto accounts (e.g., buying, selling, trading, staking, mining). If you do this, your tax lawyer, accountant, or preparer will be able to know what you did, why you did it, when you did it, and the appropriate tax treatment. Furthermore, you may even opt to do your taxes using crypto tax software.

Your cryptocurrency, crypto wallets, crypto transactions, and crypto investments are not part of an organized system that produces tax statements or forms or has a built-in accounting system.

Part of building your wealth and avoiding problems with the IRS is keeping records of your crypto transactions, holdings, and investments. To do this, you must set up an organized system in which you can input information about your crypto investments.

If you are organized, have a sound system in place, record all your transaction data, and have a clear view of your portfolio, you will do OK during tax time and not lose money due to incorrectly reporting your taxes.

CRYPTO TAX BASICS

You are required to pay taxes on your crypto gains and be permitted to deduct your losses from your income and investment gains. Currently, the IRS has no way to track your crypto tax liability fully. However, it is still possible for the IRS to know how much money you earn from crypto investments.

The US government has begun to require crypto exchanges to keep records on who sends money to whom and how much money you sent and redeemed in fiat currency. Its rationale is to prevent cryptocurrency investors from engaging in illegal transactions and funding terrorism. To do this, they have begun requiring the crypto exchanges to report on redeemed cryptocurrency and maintain records about the transactions cashed out on the crypto exchange.

Because you are a beginner crypto investor, we will focus on the crypto taxes you will most likely have to pay: capital gains and ordinary income tax. Note that cryptocurrency is treated like property by the IRS.

A capital gains tax even occurs when you sell a security at a profit. If you have held the security for less than a year, it's a short-term capital gain treated like income. However, owning the cryptocurrency for more than a year before selling it is a long-term capital gain. Therefore, long-term capital gains are taxed at a lower rate than income.

The long-term capital gains tax rate is based on your income tax bracket and can be either at 0%, 15%, or 20% at the federal level. In addition, higher-income taxpayers may be subject to the 3.8% Net Investment Income Tax on their capital gains or other payment.

TAXABLE CRYPTO TRANSACTIONS

Trading Cryptocurrency

When you buy cryptocurrency using fiat currency, it is not a taxable event. However, if you trade one cryptocurrency for another, such as trading one crypto token for a different kind of crypto token (e.g., buying Ether with Bitcoin), this is considered a taxable event. In addition, if the value of your assets has increased due to the crypto trade, the gains may be taxable.

Redeeming Cryptocurrency

A taxable event is triggered if you redeem your cryptocurrency for fiat currency, precious metals or gems, real estate, or other assets. If you profit when your crypto is redeemed (sold for more than you paid), you must pay taxes on your capital gains. However, you can use the losses to reduce your capital gains tax or income tax if you lose money selling your cryptocurrency (sell it for less than you paid for it).

Taxable Ordinary Income

Your gains are taxed as ordinary income if you are paid or rewarded in cryptocurrency for services performed or goods provided. For example, if you are paid in cryptocurrency by your job, the funds are taxed as ordinary income. Moreover, any income you earn from staking and mining cryptocurrency is considered ordinary income. In addition, any cryptocurrency awarded to you as a reward for your staking and mining activities is taxed as ordinary income.

Spending Cryptocurrency on Goods and Services

Cryptocurrency spent to pay for goods and services may be taxed as ordinary income or capital gains, depending on when you bought and spent the crypto tokens. Such payments may include money spent creating smart contracts, payment of blockchain transaction fees, payment of crypto-related services, and anything else that can be justified as a reasonable crypto-related expense.

Non-Taxable Crypto Events

Some crypto transactions do not trigger the payment of crypto taxes. When engaging in these transactions, you must keep excellent records so that your tax lawyer/accountant can adequately account for each crypto event, and you can provide written evidence of it if the IRS audits you.

- Donations

Suppose you donate your cryptocurrency and do not receive any services, goods, or other things of value in exchange. In that case, you can claim your crypto donation as a charitable tax deduction, provided your donation is to a 501(c)(3) charity.

- Gifts

You can gift cryptocurrency to family members and others and not pay taxes on the gift. However, the amount you can gift to a recipient has a lifetime limit.

- Buying and Holding Crypto

For those who choose to buy and hold (AKA HODL) cryptocurrency, the IRS does not require you to pay any taxes on your purchased cryptocurrency until you sell it or trade it. Instead, your taxes will be based on how long you held the cryptocurrency, the difference between your capital gains and losses that year, tax deductions, and the ordinary tax income rate.

- Transferring Crypto between Crypto Wallets/Accounts

Transferring your cryptocurrency between different crypto wallets/accounts is not a taxable event. So, moving your crypto tokens from a centralized exchange to your crypto wallet does not trigger a tax event, nor does moving your cryptocurrency from crypto wallet to crypto wallet trigger a tax event.

POTENTIALLY TAXABLE CRYPTO TRANSACTIONS

- Salaries paid in cryptocurrency
- Payment for goods and services in cryptocurrency (e.g., transfer fees)
- Redeeming crypto tokens for fiat currency
- Using crypto tokens to pay for goods and services
- Interest earned from P2P crypto loans
- Crypto tokens earned from mining, staking, and liquidity pools

- Referral rewards (e.g., Binance referral)
- Crypto tokens received from Learn to Earn campaigns (e.g., Coinbase Earn, CoinMarketCap Earn)
- Crypto earned from watch-to-earn platforms (e.g., Odyssey)
- Crypto earned from browsing-to-earn platforms (e.g., Permission.io browser extension, Brave browser)
- Crypto tokens earned from play-to-earn (P2E) games
- Crypto earned from shop-to-earn platforms (e.g., Lolli)
- Crypto earned from shared public address to earn platforms (e.g., Moon Faucet)
- Buying crypto tokens with stablecoins
- Transfer fees charged for moving crypto between crypto wallets
- Crypto tokens acquired via airdrops and blockchain hard forks
- Tokens and fiat currency received from selling, trading, and spending crypto tokens acquired via airdrops and blockchain hard forks
- Transactions in which you are gifted tokens you redeem, trade, and use to pay for goods and services

TAX-FREE CRYPTO TRANSACTIONS

Crypto holders are not required to pay taxes on the following transactions:

- Buying crypto tokens using fiat currency (e.g., USD, GBP, JPY, EUR)
- HODLing crypto
- Transferring crypto between crypto wallets (however, wallet transfer fees may be taxable)
- Donating crypto to 501(c)(3)-approved charities
- Gifting crypto tokens to others under the following conditions:

- May gift up to $15,000 in 2021 and $16,000 in 2022
- Must be under the lifetime gift limit per recipient, $11.7 million in 2021 and $12.16 million in 2022
- Creating NFTs

Note: Additionally, no taxes are assessed for blockchain soft forks, because platform users don't receive new tokens when soft forks are launched.

PROHIBITED CAPITAL GAINS LOSSES

Lost or stolen crypto cannot be claimed as a crypto capital gains losses.

FULL INVESTMENT WRITE-OFF

It may be possible to completely write off crypto tokens that have lost all their value (e.g., Luna). If your crypto tokens are "dead," not likely to be revived (i.e., have value), and you burn them in a dead wallet, you can write off the entire loss without being limited by the annual $3,000 deduction cap. Note that if the "dead token" revives itself, the whole investment write-off will not be allowed by the IRS.

TAX DEDUCTIONS ON CRYPTO SOLD AT A LOSS

If you sell your crypto tokens at a loss and have held them for less than a year, you can deduct the loss from your short-term gains first and then from your long-term profits. Likewise, any long-term crypto capital losses must first be used against your long-term crypto capital gain and then against your short-term capital gains.

UNSETTLED CRYPTO TAX ISSUES

- Tax treatment of crypto earned from Proof of Stake and DeFi protocols.
- The IRS has not made it clear whether you can add fees paid for crypto transfers from wallet to wallet to the cost basis of the crypto token.

WASH-SALE RULE & ITS RISKS

For traditional stock investments, if you want to take a deduction for selling your stocks at a loss, you cannot sell the stock and repurchase it at a lower price within 30 days. Likewise, if you buy back the same stock you sell at a loss within 30 days, you will not be allowed to deduct the loss from your taxes.

In the case of crypto assets, the IRS has not banned selling crypto at a loss and rebuying the same crypto tokens when the price is low within a 30-day period. However, if you do this, the IRS can audit you. If the IRS audits you and the IRS decides that your crypto transactions lack "economic substance," then you will not be allowed to use the deductions to offset your tax obligations.

Ultimately, you must decide if you are willing to risk an IRS audit because of repurchasing the crypto tokens you sold at a loss less than 30 days after you sold them—or whether you are ready to forego the potential profit you could earn by rebuying the crypto you sold at a loss in less than 30 days.

SHORT-TERM VS. LONG-TERM CAPITAL GAINS TAX SCHEDULE

Short-Term Capital Gains Definition

· · ·

Short-term capital gains are profits from assets sold less than a year after you acquired them and taxed as ordinary income. For example, profits earned by day traders who hold their crypto tokens for less than a year are taxed as regular income.

If disposal of your crypto tokens qualifies as a short-term capital gain/loss, then it will be treated like ordinary income. Therefore, you should add the gains/profits to your ordinary income and deduct the losses from your ordinary income.

The federal ordinary tax schedules for 2021 and 2022 are listed below.

Long-Term Capital Gains Definition

Long-term capital gains are assets that are sold (e.g., redeemed for fiat currency, traded, or used to pay for goods and services) after being held for a year or more. They are taxed at 0%, 15%, and 20%, depending on your ordinary income tax bracket and capital gains for the tax year.

The long-term capital gains tax schedules are listed below.

The 0% tax rate only applies if the taxpayer's ordinary income and capital gains are less than the maximum amount listed in the 0% tax bracket.

General Crypto Tax Information

- All crypto transactions that are taxable events you must report to the IRS.
- When you transfer crypto between wallets, HODL

crypto, donate crypto to a 501(c)(3) charity, give crypto as a gift (some conditions apply), or buy crypto with fiat currency, you are not required to pay taxes on those transactions.

- All major crypto exchanges licensed in the US must complete Know Your Customer (KYC) protocols on their platform users.
- Crypto exchanges collect and store your banking information when you buy crypto tokens using fiat currency.
- Crypto exchanges match custodial crypto wallets to their owners when you transfer crypto tokens into your custodial wallets at the exchange.
- Many crypto exchanges are sending 1099s to the IRS and their platform users.
- Crypto tokens are considered property by the IRS. When you sell, trade, or use crypto to pay for goods and services, you must pay taxes on the transactions, and you must pay capital gains and income taxes.
- The IRS has won lawsuits against several crypto exchanges (e.g., Kraken, Poloniex, Coinbase). The judges in those cases ruled that the crypto exchanges had to share their platform users' data with the IRS.

GENERAL CRYPTO TAX REPORTING BASICS

When determining your tax liability for the tax year, you must be careful to do the following:

- Carefully review the details regarding each of your crypto transactions.
- Know the cost basis (original purchase price) of each crypto token.
- Know the fair market value (FMV) of each crypto token.

- Calculate whether you earned a profit or suffered a loss when you disposed of each crypto token.
- Identify whether each transaction should be allocated as a long-term or short-term capital gain/loss.
- Fill out the correct tax forms and file them with the IRS (with the required supporting documentation).
- Keep your crypto records for at least 6 years, because the IRS can audit you for up to 6 years after filing your taxes.

Determining the Cost Basis of a Crypto Token

The cost basis of a token is its cost to you on the day you acquire the token. If you have cryptocurrencies awarded to you (e.g., airdropped) from your crypto investments, then you must use the FMV of the token at the time it was awarded. For tokens that were gifted or donated to you (or your organization), you would use the cost basis recorded by the original crypto token holder or the FMV of the crypto token the day it was gifted/donated to you.

Please note that you can only use one accounting method for crypto transactions. The types of accounting systems most often used by crypto holders are First In First Out (FIFO), Last In First Out (LIFO), Highest In First Out (HIFO), and specified date of acquisition.

Please consult with a crypto tax accountant, lawyer, or crypto tax professional (e.g., tax preparer, bookkeeper). They can explain the advantages and disadvantages of each type of accounting method.

To make it easier to record your taxable crypto transactions, determine whether the transactions should be taxed as capital gains or ordinary income, and file the appropriate tax forms.

PAYING CRYPTO TAXES

Your crypto taxes are due when you pay your annual income tax. However, suppose you are subject to another tax arrangement (e.g., overseas taxpayers). In that case, you should consult a tax accountant or lawyer to determine how you should pay your crypto taxes. A crypto tax professional can help you avoid potential penalties and interest due to you being delinquent on your tax obligations.

TAX FORMS YOU NEED TO KNOW

Form 8949

- **Who Files:** Taxpayers who have capital gains or losses during the financial year.
- **Information Needed:** Must enter all crypto disposal data. You must separate the data into short-term and long-term holding periods.

Schedule D (Form 1040)

- **Who Files:** Taxpayers who have capital gains or losses during the tax year.
- **Information Needed:** The form summarizes Form 8949 and contains the total short-term and long-term capital gains/losses for the tax year.

Schedule 1 (Form 1040)

- **Who Files:** Taxpayers who have received some form of income from cryptocurrencies during the tax year.
- **Information Needed:** Must enter your total additional income from crypto transactions on Line 8 of the form.

FBAR (Report of Foreign Bank and Financial Accounts)

- **Who Files:** Taxpayers with fiat currency or specified foreign financial assets worth more than $10,000 in combined value in non-US exchanges at any time during the tax year must file FBAR.
- **Information Needed:** Must enter details about your foreign exchange accounts and the maximum fiat value you had on them during the tax year.

FATCA (Foreign Account Tax Compliance Act)

- **Who Files:** Taxpayers with fiat currency or specified foreign financial assets worth more than $50,000 on the last day of the tax year or more than $75,000 at any time during the tax year in a non-US exchange. Note that this form is only needed if you hold fiat currency during the tax year. You don't need to file this form if all your crypto transactions are done using crypto tokens and stablecoins.
- **Information Needed:** Must enter details about your foreign exchange accounts with information about the

maximum value of fiat currency and ending balance during the tax year.

FILING YOUR CRYPTO TAXES

If you have a good handle or a minimal number of cryptocurrency transactions, you can manually fill out Form 8949. However, suppose you have made many cryptocurrency transactions throughout the year on multiple exchanges and used numerous wallets. In that case, it might be quite a lengthy task to stitch all the transactions together to determine your gains or losses. So instead, you can leverage an online crypto tax service that helps you stitch all the cryptocurrency transactions together and automatically generate Form 8949.

MANUALLY FILING YOUR CRYPTO TAXES

- Complete Form 8949. To do this, you must enter all taxable crypto you disposed of during the tax year.
- Report all your net crypto capital gains and losses from Form 8949 on Form Schedule D (includes short-term and long-term gains and losses).
- Report your crypto income from airdrops and blockchain hard forks, liquidity pools, bonuses, referral rewards, etc., on Form Schedule 1.
- Taxpayers who are self-employed or running a crypto business and have crypto income must complete Form Schedule C.
- Complete your tax return, Form 1040, and attach the other forms you completed to your tax filing.
- File the completed forms with the IRS.

USING A CRYPTOCURRENCY ONLINE TAX PREPARATION SOFTWARE

You can reference the appendix section in this book for recommendations on cryptocurrency tax filing software. But to prepare for using the online tax software, you need to organize all your transaction data in one place. See the recommendations below on creating a folder file system to consolidate all your cryptocurrency exchange and wallet transaction details.[19]

MANAGE RAW CRYPTOCURRENCY TRANSACTIONAL DATA

1. Download all your transaction data for your cryptocurrency exchanges and wallets.
2. Create a folder called "Tax Year" in that folder. In the "Tax Year" folder, create folders for each crypto exchange you worked with during that year. The DOWNLOADED-RAW folder will contain all the transaction data you downloaded directly from the exchange or wallet. The idea is to have the downloaded data completely unmodified. The MODIFIED-IMPORT folder will contain any formatting changes required by the tax software for it to be correctly imported.

Example:
2022 / Coinbase / DOWNLOADED-RAW
2022 / Coinbase / MODIFIED-IMPORT
2022 / EXODUS-WALLET / DOWNLOADED-RAW
2022 / EXODUS-WALLET / MODIFIED-IMPORT

Within each MODIFIED-IMPORT folder, include the transaction data for the year using the file name format {exchange/wallet}-{tax year}-{today's date in mm-dd-yy}-IMPORT.xls

. . .

Example: Coinbase-2022-04-01-2023-IMPORT.xls

Do not change the file name for the files downloaded from the exchange or wallet in the DOWNLOADED-RAW folder. An example of what the cryptocurrency exchange or wallet stores in the transaction logs (e.g., column headings):

- Date (format) (e.g., 01 Jan 2022 12:00:00 GMT)
- Transaction Type (Buy/Sell/Trade/Mining Rewards)
- Number of Coins Sold
- Price of Coin Sold
- Name of Coin Sold
- Number of Coins Bought
- Coin Name Bought
- Price of Coin Bought in USD (Cost Basis)
- Transaction Fees
- Cryptocurrency Exchange
- Jurisdiction in which crypto exchange is based (e.g., US, Canada, Switzerland)

Archive all your transaction data into these folders, and when tax time comes around, you will have a repository of all your tax data that you can import into the tax software. The cryptocurrency tax software will automatically generate your Form 8949, which you can then send to your accountant or use software that can complete it. You must submit all forms to the IRS. Consider TurboTax and TaxAct.

CREATE YOUR CRYPTOCURRENCY MASTER PORTFOLIO

An excellent way to keep track of your overall cryptocurrency holdings, gains, and losses throughout the year is to record them in a master portfolio. Then, you can quickly reference them if your crypto tax professional has questions on each transaction's classification and needs further calculations on gains or losses required to complete the required tax forms.

The process of creating a master portfolio is described below:

- Create a master portfolio using the cryptocurrency portfolio service to view your total number of crypto tokens and their value. You can reference the Cryptocurrency Charting and Portfolio services in the appendix. Some of these websites provide free services, such as CoinGecko.com.
- Accurately record all your transactions on a coin tracking website, which will keep you updated on your portfolio and help you plan your next strategic market move.

CONCLUSION

What a swell journey of cryptocurrency discovery we just went on! It's been quite a ride since we began in the first chapter. First, we started with a secret blueprint to help put you in the right mindset for your cryptocurrency investing adventure and quickly build your foundational knowledge. We learned first to decide that we want to make cryptocurrency investing primarily serve the purpose we want and that we will not doubt ourselves and let our emotions control our decisions. In addition, we went over the many benefits and opportunities currently and quickly becoming available to us via cryptocurrency. Once we decided to make cryptocurrency investing a tool for achieving the goals we wanted, we started to build the fundamental knowledge to help us wield this new financial tool.

To help build your foundational knowledge of cryptocurrency, we traveled back in time to see how societies and nations have traditionally used objects as a store of wealth. And as we move to more modern times, the solution is vastly becoming digital. Understanding how countries keep the value of wealth through currency over time and all the different challenges these currencies underwent is the first step to gaining perspective and insight into helping you evaluate and find a winning blockchain and cryptocurrency you can invest in confidently. For example, we see the negative impact of high inflation in our current fiat system. We can now look for cryptocurrencies with a finite number of minted coins, whereby the coin's value may be ever-increasing due to supply and demand. We can also see that not only is having a limited number of coins minted an essential factor, but now we can also analyze how the coins are distributed and how much of the coin is burned to determine the viability of a cryptocurrency. In addition, we can see the vast importance of having faster transaction speeds and the robust-ness of the blockchain to endure all the challenges a currency system faces. A top-tier blockchain that can quickly process transactions, consistently make plans to increase transaction speed, and has limited or no downtime is a sure long-term win.

Additionally, we see how revolutionary blockchains are by their decentralized, cryptographic, consensus-driven algorithms and immutable ledger characteristics. All of these critical charac-teristics help make cryptocurrency virtually unconfiscatable and secure. Moreover, we can see how the blockchain creates trust without needing a third party by having a public ledger and allowing peer-to-peer transactions. All these unique features of this revolutionary technology are second to none and are helping re-shape the world we know positively. In addition to learning about the revolutionary blockchain technology, we learned how to set up our first cryptocurrency account on Coinbase and safely secure and store our newly purchased coins in non-custodial wallets. Non-custodial means it is in our possession, and no one can take it away from us. It's one of the keys to creating multi-generational wealth and a key pillar in asset diversification and security. Finally, we learned about different cryptocurrency wallets' unique characteristics. Each type of wallet offers extra flexibility and security to fit your cryptocurrency needs.

Furthermore, we looked at ways to evaluate and choose cryp-tocurrency exchanges and the differences between a centralized and decentralized exchange. More importantly, we discovered ways to safeguard our cryptocurrencies from scammers or hackers looking for ways to access our private keys. So, if someone famous e-mails you asking you to share your private key to enter a sweepstake, now you know to *stay far away*! We also learned to secure our crypto investments by not falling for shilling scams or buying into a scammer's asymmetrical give-away. If it's too good to be true, it's probably not true.

All this fundamental knowledge is critical when you embark on your crypto adventure. You don't want to miss out on these ways to protect your digital assets, or it will be a very costly experience.

We then evaluated ways to invest in cryptocurrency through fundamental and technical analysis. For technical analysis, if you spend time and practice reading candlestick charts for bullish or bearish indicators, it will help you develop your trading skills and give you new insights into making crypto investments a way to achieve your financial goals and dreams. We then came to the crucial and exciting topic of the possibility and opportunity of generating multi-generational wealth by leveraging the unique features of the blockchain. Mass adoption has not occurred with cryptocurrencies, and its substantial multiplier effects are still broadly available. In sum, the blockchain revolution and the availability of these investment multipliers have created a unique opportunity where the average person can generate substantial wealth and pass it to the next generation.

Lastly, we took the necessary precautionary steps to learn about cryptocurrency taxation and the importance of consolidating and organizing all your exchange transaction logs so that you are ready to generate the required tax documentation for your accountant when tax season comes around. In addition, we learned about ways to manage our taxes, so we don't spend countless hours creating tax reports. Now we can avoid all the headaches by continually building an overview portfolio to track our cryptocurrency gains and losses.

Finally, I implore you to take action! Continue your cryptocurrency discovery journey and keep building your investing skillsets and expertise. I promise, as we said in the beginning, once you decide, put in the effort, get the best information, and keep practicing, you will get better and better at reaching your financial and personal goals. You will have tremendous ability to make a revolutionary technology of our time serve your financial purposes, goals, and dreams.

On behalf of the team here, we are committed to bringing the highest quality materials to our customers. We went to great lengths to ensure that the content of this book contains the most crucial information to help you on your cryptocurrency discovery journey and exceed your expectations. We hope you enjoyed it! We sincerely thank you for your time and investment in this book. Online reviews are immensely important to us in this digital world. We would be extremely grateful if you would take a moment to provide some feedback on our book on Amazon. It's a quick and easy way for you to make a big difference for us!

Cryptocurrency Wallets

SOFTWARE WALLETS

ATOMICWALLET.IO

BITFI.COM

COINOMI.COM

CRYPTO.COM

EXODUS.COM

KEPLR.APP

HARDWARE WALLETS

KEEPKEY

TREZOR

LEDGER

Cryptocurrency Charting & Portfolio Services

COIN360.COM

COINGECKO.COM

COINCHECKUP.COM

COINMARKETCAP.COM

COINTRACKING.COM

CRYPTOWAT.CH

TRADINGVIEW.COM

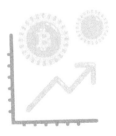

Cryptocurrency Youtubers

ALTCOIN DAILY

BITCOIN BEN

BITBOY CRYPTO

COIN BUREAU

CRYPTOSRUS

JSNIP4 (REALIST NEWS)

ROADTOROOTA

Cryptocurrency Exchanges

BINANCE.US

BLOCKFI.COM

COINBASE.COM

CRYPTO.COM

ETORO.COM

GEMINI.COM

HUOBI.COM

KRAKEN.COM

KUCOIN.COM

PIONEX.COM

POLONIEX.COM

Cryptocurrency Decentralized Exchanges (DEX)

OASIS.APP

OSMOSIS.APP

PANCAKESWAP.FINANCE

PARASAWP.IO

PSTAKE.FINANCE

UNISWAP.ORG

SUSHI.COM

TRADERJOEXYZ.COM

RAYDIUM.IO

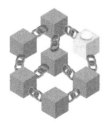

Cryptocurrency Tax Software

ACCOINTING.COM

BITCOIN.TAX

KOINLY.IO

COINTRACKER.IO

COINLEDGER.IO

TOKENTAX.CO

ZENLEDGER.IO

References

1. Craig, Jeffrey. "What Is Transactions Per Second (TPS): A Comparative Look at Networks." *Phemex*, November 2, 2021. https://phemex.com/blogs/what-is-transactions-per-second-tps.

2. Voigt, Kevin. "11 Best Crypto Exchanges and Apps of August 2022." NerdWallet, August 1, 2022. https://www.nerdwallet.com/best/investing/crypto-exchanges-platforms.

3. "All You Need to Know about 2^256." Talkcrypto.org, April 8, 2019. http://www.talkcrypto.org/blog/2019/04/08/all-you-need-to-know-about-2256/.

4. Jančis, Mindaugas. "How to Create a Good and Strong Password." *Cybernews*, August 4, 2022. https://cybernews.com/best-password-managers/how-to-create-a-strong-password/.

5. Wikipedia. 2013. *Candlestick Chart Scheme*. May 12, 2013. Originally By Probe-Meteo.com. https://commons.wikimedia.org/w/index.php?curid=26048221.

6. Hoerning, Joshua. *How to Read Candlesticks*. April 2021. Illustration. Financial Freedom Trading, April 9, 2021. https://flickr.com/photos/192693389@N04/51105447007/.

7. Hassan, Mohamed Mahmoud. *Stock Candle Chart*. 2022. Illustration. PublicDomainPictures, 2022. https://www.publicdomainpictures.net/en/view-image.php?image=360525&picture=stock-candle-chart.

8. Hoerning, Joshua. *Strength of Candlesticks*. April 2021. Illustration. Financial Freedom Trading, April 8, 2021. https://flickr.com/photos/192693389@N04/51104799010/.

9. Hoerning, Joshua. *Bullish Candlesticks*. April 2021.

Illustration. Financial Freedom Trading, April 9, 2021.
https://flickr.com/photos/192693389@N04/51105745159/.

10. Hoerning, Joshua. *Bearish Candlesticks*. April 2021.
Illustration. Financial Freedom Trading, April 10,
2021.
https://flickr.com/photos/192693389@N04/51106791340/.

11. Hoerning, Joshua. *How to Trade the Head & Shoulders
Pattern*. April 2021. Illustration. Financial Freedom
Trading, April 10, 2021. https://flickr.com/photos/192693389@N04/51106799780/

12. Crypto News, June 10, 2019. https://flickr.com/photos/163474821@N05/48036465026/.

13. Hoerning, Joshua. *Major & Minor Support and
Resistance*. April 2021. Illustration. Freedom Trading,
April 8, 2021. https://flickr.com/photos/192693389@N04/51105743469/.

14. *Breakout Patterns*. April 2021. Illustration. Financial
Freedom Trading, April 9, 2021.
https://flickr.com/photos/192693389@N04/51102543171/.

15. Newbery, Emma. "68 of the Biggest Cryptos Gained
1,000% or More in 2021." The Ascent, December 24,
2021. https://www.fool.com/the-ascent/cryptocurrency/articles/68-of-the-biggest-cryptos-gained-1000-or-more-in-2021/.

16. Nakaboto, Satoshi. "Satoshi Nakaboto: 'There Are
Now 18,000 Bitcoin Millionaires.'" *The Next Web*,
August 20, 2019. https://thenextweb.com/news/satoshi-nakaboto-there-are-now-18000-bitcoin-millionaires.

17. Napoletano, E. "How to Invest with Dollar Cost
Averaging." *Forbes Advisor*, February 10, 2022.
https://www.forbes.com/advisor/investing/dollar-cost-averaging/.

18. Jsnip4. "Realist News." Patreon. https://www.patreon.com/jsnip4.

19. Phillips, Kirk. Online course by TheBitcoinCPA. https://www.thebitcoincpa.com/.

Bibliography

1. "The History of Money." *Nova*, October 26, 1996. https://www.pbs.org/wgbh/nova/article/history-money/.
2. Neosperience Team. "10 Ways the Internet has Changed the Way We Love (And Do Business)." *Neosperience*, May 1, 2021. https://www.neosperience.com/blog/10-ways-the-internet-has-changed-the-way-we-live-and-do-business/.
3. Zaman, Uneesa. "How Cryptomarkets Revolutionised Financial Freedom." *Raconteur*, March 22, 2021. https://www.raconteur.net/finance/cryptocurrency/crypto-financial-freedom/.
4. Hussain, Sajjad. "How to Achieve Financial Freedom with Cryptocurrency." *Medium*, April 24, 2021. https://medium.com/cryptocurrencies-ups-and-down/how-to-achieve-financial-freedom-with-cryptocurrency-5c2de89aa09.
5. Prypto. "Financial Freedom Offered by Bitcoin." Dummies.com, August 29, 2016. https://www.dummies.com/article/business-careers-money/personal-finance/cryptocurrency/financial-freedom-offered-bitcoin-223555/.
6. "Can Crypto Really Replace Your Bank Account?" Coinbase. https://www.coinbase.com/learn/crypto-basics/can-crypto-really-replace-your-bank.
7. "Cryptocurrency Is All about Freedom." *Bitcoinist*, https://bitcoinist.com/cryptocurrency-is-all-about-freedom/.
8. "Why Cryptocurrency is the Future of Humanity." *Medium*, August 27, 2021.

https://ceek.medium.com/why-cryptocurrency-is-
the-future-of-humanity-38b8be154ff0.

9. Scott, Elizabeth. "What Is the Law of Attraction?"
VeryWellMind, August 8, 2022. https://www.very-
wellmind.com/understanding-and-using-the-law-of-
attraction-3144808.

10. Lielacher, Alex. "How to Invest in Tokenized Stocks
Using Trust Wallet." Trust Wallet, November 10, 2021.
https://trustwallet.com/blog/how-to-invest-in-
tokenized-stocks.

11. "Crypto Derivatives 101: A Beginner's Guide on
Crypto Futures, Crypto Options and Perpetual
Contracts." CoinTelegraph. https://cointelegraph.-
com/trading-for-beginners/crypto-derivatives-101-a-
beginners-guide-on-crypto-futures-crypto-options-
and-perpetual-contracts.

12. "What Are Crypto Exchange Traded Products?" Ficas.
https://ficas.com/blog/crypto-exchange-traded-
products/.

13. "Fiat Money vs. Cryptocurrency." Gemini, June 28,
2022. https://www.gemini.com/cryptopedia/fiat-vs-
crypto-digital-currencies.

14. Mehta, Rishi. "Hashing Algorithms, the Brain of
Blockchain (SHA-256, SHA-512 and More)." *Medium*,
August 18, 2019. https://medium.com/@rishi30-
mehta/hashing-algorithms-the-brain-of-blockchain-
sha-256-sha-512-and-more-7b5f80b99b00.

15. Hooper, Anatol. "Transaction Fees, Explained."
Cointelegraph, November 2, 2020. https://cointele-
graph.com/explained/transaction-fees-explained.

16. Spade, Jack. "A Complete History of Bitcoin Forks."
CryptoVantage, June 16, 2022. https://www.crypto-
vantage.com/guides/a-complete-history-of-bitcoin-
forks/.

17. "What is a DEX (Decentralized Exchange)?"

Chainlink, May 10, 2022. https://blog.chain.link/dex-decentralized-exchange/.

18. Frankenfield, Jake. "Initial Coin Offering (ICO)." *Investopedia*, July 7, 2022. https://www.investopedia.com/terms/i/initial-coin-offering-ico.asp.

19. Wood, Jackson. "Understanding DeFi and Its Importance in the Crypto Economy." *CoinDesk*, January 20, 2022. https://www.coindesk.com/tech/2022/01/20/understanding-defi-and-its-importance-in-the-crypto-economy.

20. Little, Kendall. "Want to Buy Crypto? Here's What to Look for in a Crypto Exchange." *NextAdvisor*, May 3, 2022. https://time.com/nextadvisor/investing/cryptocurrency/what-are-cryptocurrency-exchanges/.

21. "What Are Single-Chain and Multi-Chain Wallets." *Medium*, May 14, 2019. https://medium.com/@support_34903/what-are-single-chain-and-multi-chain-wallets-dc0ce4f21f71.

22. Lielacher, Alex. "Hot Wallets vs Cold Wallets: What's the Difference?" *Alexandria*, 2021. https://coinmarketcap.com/alexandria/article/hot-wallets-vs-cold-wallets-whats-the-difference.

23. Rosson, Maxi. "The Best Ways to Protect the Seed Phrases of Your Crypto Wallets." *Medium*, April 15, 2022. https://medium.com/the-crypto-bookstore/the-best-ways-to-protect-the-seed-phrases-of-your-wallets-150bb10ea1da.

24. Bitcoin Wiki. 2022. "Seed Phrase." July 12, 2022. https://en.bitcoin.it/wiki/Seed_phrase.

25. "What is Two-Factor Authentication (2FA)?" Authy. https://authy.com/what-is-2fa/.

26. Lodha, Chandan. "2022 Crypto-Exchange Fee Comparison." CoinTracker, July 22, 2022. https://www.cointracker.io/blog/2019-crypto-exchange-fee-comparison.

27. "The Ultimate Guide on Cryptocurrency Security." *Medium*, November 3, 2021. https://fintelics.medium.com/the-ultimate-guide-on-cryptocurrency-security-7738d1aafc74.
28. "9 Ways to Keep Your Crypto Safe." *Medium*, September 30, 2021. https://medium.com/coinmonks/9-ways-to-keep-your-crypto-safe-d969aa791070.
29. "Crypto Security 101: Securing Your Wallet." *Medium*, February 20, 2022. https://noahjd.medium.com/crypto-security-101-securing-your-wallet-d324a95c525d.
30. Samuel, Andy. "How to Password Protect a Flash Drive? 3 Easy Ways Here." PassFab, November 28, 2020. https://www.passfab.com/password/how-to-password-protect-usb-flash-drive.html.
31. Jančis, Mindaugas. "How to Create a Good and Strong Password." *Cybernews*, August 4, 2022. https://cybernews.com/best-password-managers/how-to-create-a-strong-password/.
32. Sarkar, Arijit. "Trezor Investigates Potential Data Breach as Users Cite Phishing Attacks." Cointelegraph, April 3, 2022. https://cointelegraph.com/news/trezor-investigates-potential-data-breach-as-users-cite-phishing-attacks.
33. "What Happened to Mt. Gox? Who Stole the Bitcoins?" Productmint. https://productmint.com/what-happened-to-mt-gox/.
34. Ferber, Lisa. "How Crypto Investors Can Avoid the Scam that Captured $2.8 Billion in 2021." *NextAdvisor*, April 19, 2022. https://time.com/nextadvisor/investing/cryptocurrency/protect-yourself-from-crypto-pump-and-dump/.
35. "What is Fundamental Analysis in Crypto Trading?" *Medium*, September 17, 2021. https://medi-

um.com/exmo-official/what-is-fundamental-analysis-in-crypto-trading-b72a25bf1ba8.

36. "How to Do Technical Analysis for Cryptocurrency." *Medium*, March 11, 2021. https://medium.com/stormgain-crypto/how-to-do-technical-analysis-for-cryptocurrency-e1ae6d3f7665.

37. Hussey, Matt. "Who Are the Fastest Growing Developer Communities in Crypto?" *Decrypt*, April 16, 2021. https://decrypt.co/66740/who-are-the-fastest-growing-developer-communities-in-crypto.

38. "What is Market Capitalisation (Market Cap) and Why Does It Matter?" Bitpanda. https://www.bitpanda.com/academy/en/lessons/what-is-market-capitalisation-market-cap-and-why-does-it-matter/.

39. Frankenfield, Jake. "Initial Coin Offering (ICO)." Investopedia, August 18, 2022. https://www.investopedia.com/terms/i/initial-coin-offering-ico.asp.

40. "What is RSI and How Do You Apply It to Crypto Trading?" Bybit Learn, May 18, 2021. https://learn.bybit.com/indicators/what-is-rsi-and-how-do-you-apply-it-to-crypto-trading/.

41. "What is a MACD Indicator? (How to Use it in Crypto Trading)." Bybit Learn, April 3, 2021. https://learn.bybit.com/indicators/explained-macd-indicator-how-to-apply-it-in-crypto-trading/.

42. "What's the Backstory on the Word, HODL?" *Medium*, April 30, 2017. https://medium.com/hackernoon/whats-the-backstory-on-the-word-hodl-27756392b698.

43. Klemens, Sam. "How to HODL: A Guide to Saving in Bitcoin (BTC)." *Crypto News*, Exodus, May 18, 2021. https://www.exodus.com/news/guide-to-saving-in-bitcoin/.

44. "Ethereum — A Generational Investment." *Medium*, January 22, 2022. https://medium.com/@halp1120/1-

the-only-other-large-assets-that-arguably-have-structural-demand-are-luna-and-bnb-cdcf8b2a8281.

45. DiLallo, Matthew. "Understanding Portfolio Diversification." The Motley Fool, June 30, 2022. https://www.fool.com/investing/how-to-invest/portfolio-diversification/.

46. Warren, Rachel, Travis Hoium, and Connor Allen. "3 Investors Discuss Their Approach to Holding Cash in Their Portfolios." The Motley Fool, December 19, 2021. https://www.fool.com/investing/2021/12/19/3-investors-discuss-their-approach-to-holding-cash/.

47. "Use Dollar-Cost Averaging to Build Wealth Over Time." Investopedia, December 5, 2021. https://www.investopedia.com/investing/dollar-cost-averaging-pays/.

48. Daly, Lyle. "65% of Americans Make This Mistake After Investing in Crypto." The Ascent, July 17, 2021. https://www.fool.com/the-ascent/cryptocurrency/articles/65-of-americans-make-this-mistake-after-investing-in-crypto/.

49. "What is FOMO and How Does It Affect Crypto?" The Guardian, January 18, 2022. https://guardian.ng/news/what-is-fomo-and-how-does-it-affect-crypto/.

50. Brooks, Miles. "The Ultimate Crypto Tax Guide (2022)." CoinLedger, 2022. https://coinledger.io/crypto-taxes.

51. "Understanding Crypto Taxes." Coinbase, 2022. https://www.coinbase.com/learn/crypto-basics/understanding-crypto-taxes.

52. Brooks, Miles. "FIFO, LIFO, and HIFO – What's the Best Method for Crypto?" CoinLedger. https://coinledger.io/blog/cryptocurrency-tax-calculations-fifo-and-lifo-costing-methods-explained.

53. Adams, Riley. "What is an IRS 1099 Form?" TurboTax,

July 14, 2022. https://turbotax.intuit.com/tax-tips/irs-tax-forms/what-is-an-irs-1099-form/L3NxSPMUe.

54. "Managing Your Portfolio with CoinGecko: A How-To Guide." Publish0x, October 3, 2020. https://www.publish0x.com/hobbyist-crypto/managing-your-portfolio-with-coingecko-a-how-to-guide-xvrxzwj.

55. A., Julija. "Best Crypto Tax Software Solutions Reviewed." Fortunly, August 5, 2022. https://fortunly.com/investments/best-crypto-tax-software.

56. Chandrasekera, Shehan. "How to Pick the Best Crypto Tax Software." *Forbes*, January 7, 2020. https://www.forbes.com/sites/shehanchandrasekera/2020/01/07/how-to-pick-the-best-crypto-tax-software/?sh=121615bd76fb.